A GIFT FOR

_____

—•◦•—

FROM

_____

HOPE

FOR EVERY MOMENT

T.D. JAKES

DESTINY IMAGE® PUBLISHERS, INC.
P.O. Box 310, Shippensburg, PA 17257-0310
"Promoting Inspired Lives."

This book and all other Destiny Image and Destiny Image Fiction books are available at Christian bookstores and distributors worldwide.

Cover design by: Eileen Rockwell
Interior design by: Terry Clifton

For more information on foreign distributors, call 717-532-3040.
Reach us on the Internet: www.destinyimage.com.

ISBN 13 TP: 978-0-7684-1564-3
ISBN 13 eBook: 978-0-7684-1565-0
Previously Published ISBN: 978-0-7684-2397-6

For Worldwide Distribution, Printed in the U.S.A.
1 2 3 4 5 6 7 8 / 21 20 19 18 17

And, behold, there was a woman which had a spirit of infirmity eighteen years, and was bowed together, and could in no wise lift up herself...He called her to Him, and said unto her, Woman, thou art loosed from thine infirmity (LUKE 13:11-12 KJV).

———◦○◦———

Perhaps you will find some point of relativity between her case history and your own. There are three major characters in this story: the person, the problem, and the prescription. For every person, there will be a problem and for every problem, our God has a prescription!

Jesus' opening statement to this woman is not a recommendation for counseling—it is a challenging command! Jesus did not counsel what should have been commanded. I am not against seeking the counsel of godly men. The Scriptures say: *"Where there is no counsel, the people fall; but in the multitude of counselors there is safety"* (Prov. 11:14).

After you have analyzed your condition and understood its origin, it will take the authority of God's Word to put the past under your feet! Although the problem may be rooted in the past, the prescription is a present Word from God! The Word you hear today will heal your yesterday!

*But if we walk in the light as He is in the light...
the blood of Jesus Christ His Son cleanses us from
all sin* (I JOHN 1:7).

———•◦•———

The blood is the only element in the body that reaches, affects, and fuels all other parts of the body. If the blood is restricted long enough from any member of the body, that member will internally asphyxiate. Asphyxiated cells can quickly die—even without an external assailant—for their affliction is the result of internal deprivation.

Every limb and organ in the human body needs the blood. Along with its culinary duty of delivering soluble dietary contents throughout the body, our blood also functions as a paramedic. The white blood cells are uniquely equipped to fight off attacking bacteria and expel it from the body—stripping it of its power and robbing it of its spoils.

The physical body illustrates the power of the blood in the Church. Every member of the Body of Christ needs the life-giving blood of Jesus. Without the blood, we cease to have the proof of our sonship. Without His blood, we are pseudo-heirs trying to receive the promises reserved for the legitimate children of God!

To everything there is a season, and a time for every purpose under heaven (ECCLESIASTES 3:1).

We will always have seasons of struggles and testing. There are times when everything we attempt to do will seem to go wrong. Regardless of our prayers and consecration, adversity will come. We can't pray away God's seasons. The Lord has a purpose in not allowing us to be fruitful all the time. When God sends the chilly winds of winter to blow on our circumstances, we must still trust Him.

The apostle Paul calls such times *"...light affliction, which is but for a moment..."* (2 Cor. 4:17). I say, "This too shall pass!" Some things you are not meant to change, but to survive. So if you can't alter it, then outlive it! Be like a tree. In the frosty arms of winter the forest silently refurbishes its strength, preparing for its next season of fruitfulness. In the spring it will push its way up into the budding of a new experience. Temporary setbacks create opportunities for fresh commitment and renewal. There are seasons of sunshine as well as rain. Each stage has its own purpose.

For God so loved the world that He gave His only begotten Son... (JOHN 3:16).

———•◦•———

One of the first things that a hurting person needs to do is break the habit of using other people as a narcotic to numb the dull aching of an inner void. The more you medicate the symptoms, the less chance you have of allowing God to heal you. Avoid addictive, obsessive relationships.

If you are becoming increasingly dependent upon anything other than God to create a sense of wholeness in your life, then you are abusing your relationships. Clinging to people is far different from loving them. It is not so much a statement of your love for them as it is a crying out of your need for them. Like lust, it is intensely selfish. It is taking and not giving. Love is giving. God is love. God proved His love not by His need of us, but by His giving to us.

Sometimes we esteem others more important than ourselves. Watch out for self-disdain! If we don't apply some of the medicine that we use on others to strengthen ourselves, our patients will be healed and we will be dying.

...For unto obedience and sprinkling of the blood of Jesus Christ: grace to you and peace be multiplied (I PETER 1:2).

———◦———

We did not need the blood only for when we cried out to the Lord to come into our hearts by faith. On the contrary, we still need that same blood today. All our strength and nourishment and every promise and miracle must flow to us through the blood. It gives us life from day to day!

We have learned about the Spirit of God, but we failed to teach about the blood. Consequently, we are believers who are empowered but do not feel forgiven! They are operating in the gifts, but living in guilt!

The blood must be preached. Without it we have no life. Why are we wasting the power of God on the problems of our past? The blood has already totally destroyed past bondages that held us down! It was through the eternal Spirit of God that Jesus was able to offer up His blood.

Not by might nor by power, but by My Spirit, says the Lord of hosts (ZECHARIAH 4:6).

For the vision is yet for an appointed time... (HABAKKUK 2:3).

———•○•———

God is a God of order; He does everything by appointment. He has set a predetermined appointment to bring to pass His promise in our lives. Through the many tempestuous winds that blow against our lives, God has already prepared a way of escape. Our comfort is in knowing that we have an appointment with destiny. It is the inner awareness that makes us realize that in spite of temporary circumstances, God has a present time of deliverance.

We are enveloped in peace when we know that nothing the enemy does can abort the plan of God for our lives. The promise will come to pass. It will not be by human might or power, but by the Spirit of the Lord. David said, *"My times are in Your hand"* (Ps. 31:15). For me there is a sense of tranquility that comes from resting in the Lord. His appointment for us is predetermined. There is a peace that comes from knowing God has included us in His plan—even the details.

For we are His workmanship, created in Christ Jesus unto good works, which God hath before ordained that we should walk in them. (EPHESIANS 2:10 KJV).

―――――•◦•―――――

J esus knew who He was. The Lord wants to help you realize who you are and what you are graced to do. To ask someone to define you without first knowing the answer yourself is dangerous. When you understand that He is the only One who really knows you, then you pursue Him with fierceness and determination. Pursue Him.

God knows who we are and how we are to attain our calling. This knowledge, locked up in the counsel of God's omniscience, is the basis of our pursuit, and it is the release of that knowledge that brings immediate transformation. He knows the hope or the goal of our calling. He is not far removed from us; He reveals Himself to people who seek Him. The finders are the seekers. The door is opened only to the knockers and the gifts are given to the askers! (See Luke 11:9.) Initiation is our responsibility. Whosoever hungers and thirsts shall be filled. Remember, in every crisis He is never far from the seeker!

Now, therefore, you are no longer strangers and foreigners, but fellow citizens with the saints and members of the household of God (EPHESIANS 2:19).

———❖———

There is a devilish prejudice in the Church that denies the blood to its uncomely members. If a person has a failure in an area we relate to because we have a similar weakness, we immediately praise God for the blood that cleanses us from all unrighteousness. If they are unfortunate enough to fail where we are very strong, then we deny them the blood.

We have spilled our brother's blood because he is different, because his sin is different from ours. But by the blood of the Lamb, any man, regardless of his failures or past sin, can come equally and unashamedly to the foot of the Cross and allow the drops of Jesus' blood to invigorate the soul that sin has lacerated and destroyed.

Have you ever been guilty of having a condescending attitude about another person's weakness? How can we dare to think we can access the soul-cleansing blood that delivers us from the cesspool of our secret sins, and then look down on another member of Christ's Body in disdain?

...I am God, and there is no other; I am God, and there is none like Me, declaring the end from the beginning, and from ancient times things that are not yet done, saying, "My counsel shall stand, and I will do all My pleasure" (ISAIAH 46:9-10).

———•◦•———

At the early age of six, I knew I had an appointment with destiny and that God had a purpose for my life. Somewhere in the recesses of your mind there should be an inner knowing that directs you toward an expected end. You must be the kind of tenacious person who can speak to the enemy and tell him, "My life can't end without certain things coming to pass. It's not over until God says, 'It's over!'"

I can't say that everything I encountered in life pushed me toward my destiny. On the contrary, there were sharp contradictions as I went through my tempestuous teens. Still, I had that inner knowing. I want you to know that even if circumstances contradict purpose, purpose will always prevail! It is the opposition that clearly demonstrates to you that God is working. When all indicators say it is impossible and it still occurs, then you know God has done it again.

And He hath put a new song in my mouth, even praise unto our God: many shall see it, and fear, and shall trust in the Lord (PSALM 40:3 KJV).

———•◦•———

He will restore to you that which the cankerworm and the locust ate up (see Joel 2:25). He said, "I'm going to give it back to you." Maybe you wrestle with guilt. You feel so dirty. You've been misused and abused. The devil keeps bringing up to you your failures of the past.

I always tended to have a ministry of mercy. Perhaps it is because I've had my own pain. When you have suffered, it makes you able to relate to other people's pain. Sometimes when I minister, I find myself fighting back tears.

Once you have called out to Him, you can lift up your hands in praise. No matter what you have suffered, you can hold up your head. Regardless of who has hurt you, hold up your head! Forget how many times you've been married. Put aside those who mistreated you. It doesn't matter who you were. You can't change where you have been, but you can change where you are going.

Also for Adam and his wife the Lord God made tunics of skin, and clothed them (GENESIS 3:21).

———•○•———

Because we have offered no provision for sons and daughters who fall, many of our Adams and our Eves are hiding in the bushes. Our fallen brethren hear our message, but they cannot come out to a preacher or a crowd that merely points out their nakedness and has nothing to cover them. We need to offer the perfect sacrifice to the sons and daughters of God as well as to the world. Adam was God's son. He was fallen and he was foolish, but he was the son of God!

The blood of Christ will even reach the falling, faltering son who hides in the bushes of our churches. Who will walk the cool of the garden to find him or to cover him? Many of us are taking the first walk to discover the fallen, but they have not taken the deeper walk to cover the fallen. When God covered Adam and Eve's nakedness, He covered what He discovered with the bloody skins of an innocent animal, giving Himself the first sacrifice to atone for their sin.

And Adam knew his wife again, and she bore a son and named him Seth, "For God has appointed another seed for me instead of Abel, whom Cain killed" (GENESIS 4:25).

━━━━●•◦•●━━━━

When Eve produced what she thought to be the promised seed, there were real problems. In the heat of rage, Cain killed his brother. She was supposed to be the mother of all living and all she had raised was a corpse and its murderer.

But God unwrapped the blanket of failure and blessed her with another son. She named him "Seth." Seth means "substituted." Suddenly, as she held her new baby in her arms, she realized that God is sovereign. Eve called her third son "Seth," for she understood that if God makes a promise to bless someone, He will find a way! Even if it means appointing a substitute, He will perform His promise.

Ultimately everything God has ever said will come to pass. When we suffer loss like Eve did, we cannot allow past circumstances to abort future opportunity. If you have experienced loss in your life, God has a way of restoring things you thought you would never see again.

What shall we then say to these things? If God be for us, who can be against us? (ROMANS 8:31 KJV)

———————◆•◊•◆———————

Judas was no mistake. He was handpicked and selected. His role was crucial to the death and resurrection of Christ. No one helped Christ reach His goal like Judas. If God allowed certain types of people to come into our lives, they would hinder us from His divine purpose. A seasoned heart has been exercised by the tragedies of life. It has reduced and controlled the fatty feelings and emotions that cause us to always seek those whose actions tickle our ears.

We all want to be surrounded by a friend like John, whose loving head lay firmly on Jesus' breast. We may long for the protective instincts of a friend like Peter, who stood ready to attack every negative force that would come against Jesus. In his misdirected love, Peter even withstood Jesus to His face over His determination to die for mankind. But the truth of the matter is, Jesus could have accomplished His goal without Peter, James, or John; but without Judas He would never have reached the hope of His calling!

...but with His own blood He entered the Most Holy Place once for all, having obtained eternal redemption (HEBREWS 9:12).

———•◦•———

Before Adam could receive the covering God had provided, though, he had to disrobe himself of what he had contrived. Adam stripped himself before a holy God, admitted his tragic sins, and still maintained his position as a son in the presence of God. Adam and Eve realized that the only solution for their sin was in the perfect provision of their loving God. That same loving God now reaches out to us as we are, and refashions us into what we should become!

We hear no further mention of blame or guilt concerning the first family as they walked away from the worst moment in the history of humanity. Why? They were wrapped and protected in the provision of God.

We, too, need to have this knowledge, regardless of whom we would want to blame or belittle. The disease is sin, the wage or prognosis is death, and the antidote prescribed is the blood and the blood alone. Never forget the blood, for without it we have no good news at all!

If a man dies, shall he live again? All the days of my hard service I will wait, till my change comes (JOB 14:14).

———■•◦•■———

I t would be terrible to look back over your life and see that the many times you thought your request was denied was actually only delayed. Life will always present broken places, places of struggle and conflict. If you have a divine purpose and life has put you on hold, hang on! Stay on the line until life gets back to you. It's worth the wait to receive your answer from the Lord.

The real test of faith is in facing the silence of being on hold. Those are the suspended times of indecision. Have you felt you were on the verge of something phenomenal, that you were waiting for that particular breakthrough that seemed to be taunting you by making you wait? All of us have faced days that seemed as though God had forgotten us. These are the moments that feel like eternity. Patience gets a workout when God's answer is no answer. In other words, God's answer is not always yes or no; sometimes He says, "Not now!"

Sanctify them by Your truth. Your word is truth
(JOHN 17:17).

———◦◦◦———

You can have a complete metamorphosis through the Word of God. It has been my experience, as one who does extensive counseling in my own ministry and abroad, that many abused people, women in particular, tend to flock to legalistic churches who see God primarily as a disciplinarian. Many times the concept of fatherhood for them is a harsh code of ethics. This type of domineering ministry may appeal to those who are performance-oriented. I understand that morality is important in Christianity; however, there is a great deal of difference between morality and legalism. It is important that God not be misrepresented. He is a balanced God, not an extremist.

The glory of God is manifested only when there is a balance between grace and truth. Religion doesn't transform. Legalism doesn't transform. For the person who feels dirty, harsh rules could create a sense of self-righteousness. God doesn't have to punish you to heal you.

Believe the Word of God and be free. Jesus was a great emancipator of the oppressed. It does not matter whether someone has been oppressed socially, sexually, or racially; our Lord is an eliminator of distinctions.

But God demonstrates His own love toward us, in that while we were still sinners, Christ died for us (ROMANS 5:8).

———◦◦◦———

I can't help but wonder what would happen if we would ever love like Jesus loves. As we peel away layer by layer, as we become more comfortable with our God and our own humanity, we become increasingly transparent. We must achieve a level of honesty that will keep us from being estranged from our important relationships. We have to love and be loved by someone to the degree that we can say, "This is who I am, and it is all that I am. Love me and be patient with me. There is no telling what I will become, but today this is who I am."

When you find someone who can see your flaws and your underdeveloped character, and love you in spite of it all, you are blessed. If the only way you can love me is after I have perfected my imperfections, then you really don't love me. God loved you while you were unlovable so you would never have to hide in the bushes again! He has loved you with an everlasting love!

Wait on the Lord; be of good courage, and He shall strengthen your heart; wait, I say, on the Lord!
(PSALM 27:14)

———•○•———

It is God's timing that we must learn. He synchronizes His answers to accomplish His purpose. While traveling on a major American airline, we were told that the plane could not land and we had to wait in the air. I have often felt like that aircraft suspended in the air when God says, "Wait!"

There was a calm assurance on the faces of the flight attendants. I would have to attribute it to the fact that they had prepared for a delay. I began to wonder if we shouldn't be better prepared for those times when God puts us in a holding pattern. Do you have enough faith to assume a holding pattern and wait for the fulfillment of the promise?

You feel a deep sense of contentment when you know God has not forgotten you. I will never forget the time I went through a tremendous struggle. I thought it was an emergency. I thought I had to have an answer right then. I learned that God isn't easily spooked by what I call an emergency.

Or do you despise the riches of His goodness, forbearance, and longsuffering, not knowing that the goodness of God leads you to repentance? (ROMANS 2:4)

---•◦•---

Repentance doesn't come because of the scare tactics and threats of raging ministers who need mercy themselves. Repentance comes because of the unfailing love of a perfect God, a God who cares for the cracked vases that others would have discarded. It is His great love that causes a decision to be made in the heart: I must live for Him!

There is no way that you can see Him stand with you when all others forsake you, and not want to please Him! There is no way you can weather a storm in His loving arms and not say, "I am Yours, O Lord. Such as I have I give to You." One gaze into His holiness will bring the sinner crashing to the floor on bended knees, confessing and forsaking every issue that could have engulfed him.

In other words, God is too good for us to experience His love and then be contented to abuse that love. If nowhere else, and by no one else, you are accepted in the Beloved!

There is neither Jew or Greek [racial], *there is neither slave nor free* [social] *there is neither male nor female* [sexual]; *for you are all one in Christ Jesus* (GALATIANS 3:28).

———•○•———

Unity should not come at the expense of uniqueness of expression. We should also tolerate variance in social classes. The Church is not an elite organization for spiritual yuppies only, one that excludes other social classes.

If uniqueness is to be appreciated racially and socially, it is certainly to be appreciated sexually. Male and female are one in Christ. Yet they are unique and that uniqueness is not to be tampered with. It is a sin for a man to misrepresent himself by conducting himself as a woman. I am not merely speaking of homosexuality. I am also talking about men who are feminine in their mannerisms. It is equally sad to see a masculine woman. Nevertheless, God wants them healed, not hated!

God can appreciate our differences and still create unity. It is like a conductor who can orchestrate extremely different instruments into producing a harmonious, unified sound. Together we produce a sound of harmony that expresses the multifaceted character of God.

...work out your own salvation with fear and trembling; for it is God who works in you both to will and to do for His good pleasure (PHILIPPIANS 2:12-13).

———•◦•———

God is too good for us to experience His love and then be contented to abuse that love. Accepting the rejected is not the weakness of the Gospel; it is its strength! It is to the distraught heart that seeks so desperately for a place of refuge that we extend soft hands and tender words.

How can we then define the Church, with its rising divorce rate and afflicted leadership? The Church needs to bathe itself in its own message. We have strengths and struggles. We have boxed ourselves in and lifted ourselves up as the epitome of sanctity. But beneath our stained glass windows and padded pews lie broken hearts and torn families.

We have no right to be blessed, in ourselves. Yet He has blessed us "in spite of us." Beneath the streaming tears of a grateful heart, through our trembling lips must emerge the birthing thoughts that Christ has done it all, and that we have nothing to boast in but His precious blood alone!

For He knows our frame; He remembers that we are dust (PSALM 103:14).

———•○•———

Once while struggling to understand why God had not more readily answered one of my requests, I stumbled upon a word that brought streams into my desert.

But God remembered Noah...and He sent a wind over the earth, and the waters receded (Genesis 8:1 NIV).

The first four words were all I needed. When you realize that God knows where you are and that He will get back to you in time—what peace, what joy! Before Noah ran out of resources and provisions, God remembered him! The Lord knows where you are and He knows how much you have left in reserve. Just before you run out, God will send the wind to blow back the waters of impossibility and provide for you.

I, too, need ministry to keep my attitude from falling while I wait on the manifestation of the promise of God. Sometimes very simplistic reminders that God is still sovereign bring great joy to the heart of someone who is in a holding pattern. The comforting Spirit of God calms my fears every time He reminds me that God doesn't forget.

And being found in appearance as a man, He humbled Himself and became obedient to the point of death, even the death of the cross (PHILIPPIANS 2:8).

———●◦●———

To fully understand the precious effect of Jesus' blood, we must take a look back at Calvary's bloody banks. Look at the 33-year-old body that was filled with such youth and potential now hangs from a cross like a slab of unused meat. From His beaten back to His ripped torso, we see a wounded knight without armor. His garments lie crumbled on the ground, the object of the desires of His villainous guards who now gamble up their leisure moments, waiting on the death angel to flap his wings in the face of the Savior.

When you look at this icon of grace, remove your religious glasses and you will see a sweat-drenched, trembling, bleeding offering. He hung dying as if He were the bastard son of Mary, not the King that He was—dying like a thief in the night! That crucifixion was a debauchery and degradation so horrible that it embarrassed the sun into hiding its face and made the ground tremble at the nervous sight of the King of glory.

That He might sanctify and cleanse it with the washing of water by the word (EPHESIANS 5:26).

———•O•———

Transforming truths are brought forth through the birth canal of our diligence in seeking His face. David said, *"In Your presence is fullness of joy"* (Ps. 16:11). The answer is in the presence of God, not man! A renewing word will change your mind about your circumstance. Just when the enemy thinks he has you, transform before his very eyes!

No matter who left his impression upon you, God's Word prevails! The obstacles of past scars can be overcome by present truths. Your deliverance will not start in your circumstances; it evolves out of your mentality. As the Word of God waxes greater, the will of men becomes weaker. Turn the faucet of God's Word on high and ease your mind down into the water of profound truth. Wash away every limitation and residue of past obstacles and transform into the renewed person you were created to become. Whenever someone tells you what you can't do or be, or what you can't get or attain, tell them, "I can do all things through Christ who strengthens me" (see Phil. 4:13).

...for by faith you stand (2 CORINTHIANS 1:24).

———•○•———

The Holy Spirit is calling for the broken, infirm women to come to Jesus. He will restore and deliver. How do we come to Jesus? We come to His Body, the Church. It is in the Church that we can hear the Word of God. The Church gives us strength and nourishment. The Church is to be the place where we share our burdens and allow others to help us with them. The Spirit calls; the burdened need only heed the call.

There are three tenses of faith! When Lazarus died, Martha, his sister, said, "Lord, if You would have been here, my brother would not have died." This is historical faith. Its view is digressive. Then when Jesus said, "Lazarus will live again," his sister replied, "I know he will live in the resurrection." This is futuristic faith. It is progressive. Martha says, "But even now You have the power to raise him up again." (See John 11:21-27.)

I feel like Martha. Even now, after all you've been through, God has the power to raise you up again! This is the present tense of faith. Walk into your newness even now.

For I know the thoughts that I think toward you, says the Lord, thoughts of peace, and not of evil, to give you a future and a hope (JEREMIAH 29:11).

———◦———

When Noah had been held up long enough to accomplish what was necessary for his good, God sent the wind. There is a wind that comes from the presence of God. It blows back the hindrances and dries the ground beneath your feet. Whenever the breath of the Almighty breathes a fresh anointing on you, it is an indication of a supernatural deliverance.

Regardless of the obstacle in your life, the wind from God can bring you out. Let His wind blow down every spirit of fear and heaviness that would cause you to give up on what God has promised you. The description of the Holy Spirit says He is as *"a rushing mighty wind"* (Acts 2:2). For every mighty problem in your life, there is a mighty rushing wind! Now, a normal wind can be blocked out but the gusty wind from the Lord is too strong to be controlled. It will blow back the Red Sea. God's wind is ultra-effective against every current event in your life.

Nor give place to the devil (EPHESIANS 4:27).

———•◦•———

It is not enough to reject the enemy's plan. You must nurture the Word of the Lord. You need to draw the promise of God and the vision for the future to your breast. It is a natural law that anything not fed will die. Caution: Be sure you are nurturing what you want to grow and starving what you want to die.

As you read this, you may feel that life is passing you by. You often experience success in one area and gross defeat in others. You need a burning desire for the future, the kind of desire that overcomes past fear and inhibitions. You will remain chained to your past and all the secrets therein until you decide: Enough is enough!

I am telling you that when your desire for the future peaks, you can break out of prison. I challenge you to sit down and write 30 things you would like to do with your life and scratch them off, one by one, as you accomplish them. There is no way you can plan for the future and dwell in the past at the same time.

Who Himself bore our sins in His own body on the tree, that we, having died to sins, might live for righteousness—by whose stripes you were healed (I PETER 2:24).

—————•◦•—————

The Savior's head is pricked with the thorns of every issue that would ever rest on my mind. His hands are nailed through for every vile thing I have ever used mine to do. His feet are nailed to the tree for every illicit, immoral place you and I have ever walked! In spite of His pain and abuse, in spite of His torment and His nudity, He was still preaching as they watched Him dying—naked and not ashamed!

Why is a loincloth painted on most of the pictures I see of Jesus on the Cross? Isn't that what hinders us now? Are we, the Body of Christ, hiding beneath a loincloth that has stifled our testimony and blocked our ability to be transparent, even with one another? We have not been allowed to share our struggles as well as our successes. Beneath the loincloth of human expectation and excessive demands, many men and women are bleeding to death!

For we do not have a High Priest who cannot sympathize with our weaknesses, but was in all points tempted as we are, yet without sin (HEBREWS 4:15).

---•◦•---

Have you ever noticed how hard it is to communicate with people who will not give you their attention? Pain will not continue to rehearse itself in the life of a preoccupied, distracted person. Distracted people do not respond! Every woman has something she wishes she could forget. Forgetting isn't a memory lapse; it is a memory release! Like carbon dioxide the body can no longer use, exhale it and let it go out of your spirit.

God cares, sees, and calls the infirm to the dispensary of healing and deliverance. Like a 24-hour medical center, you can reach Him at anytime. He is touched by the feeling of your infirmity.

I pray that the Holy Spirit would roll you into the recovery room where you can fully realize that the trauma is over. I am excited to say that God never loosed anybody that He wasn't going to use mightily. May God reveal healing and purpose as we continue to seek Him.

The Lord has made bare His holy arm in the eyes of all the nations; and all the ends of the earth shall see the salvation of our God (ISAIAH 52:10).

---•○•---

Again, I see the tragedy in the fact that the loin-cloth represents all those things that are humanly imposed upon us, things that God does not require!

I resent the loincloth because it is almost prophetic of what the Church, the mystical Body of Christ, has done today. We have hidden our humanity beneath the man-made cloths of religiosity. We have covered up what God has made bare! We need no loincloth; the Body of Christ was meant to be naked and not ashamed. His provision for our nudity was His blood.

I hope you have only one defense when it is your turn to go on trial. Do not submit a loincloth for evidence; it is inadmissible. But my wounded, hurting, healing, helping, giving, and needing friend, when they try your case (and they surely will), open your mouth, clear your throat, and plead, "No additives; the blood alone!"

But the Scripture has confined all under sin, that the promise by faith in Jesus Christ might be given to those who believe (GALATIANS 3:22).

————•○•————

Many Christians experienced the new birth early in their childhood. It is beneficial to have the advantage of Christian ethics. I'm not sure what it would have been like to have been raised in the church and been insulated from worldliness and sin. Sometimes I envy those who have been able to live victoriously all of their lives. Most of us have not had that kind of life. My concern is the many persons who have lost their sensitivity for others and who suffer from spiritual arrogance. Jesus condemned the Pharisees for their spiritual arrogance, yet many times that self-righteous spirit creeps into the Church.

The fact is, we were all born in sin and shaped in iniquity. We have no true badge of righteousness that we can wear on the outside. God concluded all are in sin so He might save us from ourselves. We were born in sin, equally and individually shaped in iniquity, and not one race or sociological group has escaped the fact that we are Adam's sinful heritage.

For a righteous man may fall seven times and rise again, but the wicked shall fall by calamity (PROVERBS 24:16).

————◦◦◦————

Sometimes Christians become frustrated and withdraw from activity on the basis of personal struggles. They think it's all over, but God says not so! The best is yet to come. But if you want the Lord to come, you mustn't tell Him that you aren't planning to get up.

The whole theme of Christianity is one of rising again. However, you can't rise until you fall. Now that doesn't mean you should fall into sin. It means you should allow the resurrecting power of the Holy Ghost to operate in your life regardless of whether you have fallen into sin, discouragement, apathy, or fear. But it doesn't matter what tripped you; it matters that you rise up. People who never experience these things generally are people who don't do anything. There is a certain safety in being dormant. Nothing is won, but nothing is lost. I would rather walk on the water with Jesus. I would rather nearly drown and have to be saved than play it safe and never experience the miraculous.

To the praise of the glory of His grace, by which He made us accepted in the Beloved (EPHESIANS 1:6).

————•◦•————

I remember, in my early days as a new Christian, that I tried to become what I thought all the other Christians were. I didn't understand that my goal should have been to achieve God's purpose for my life. I was young and so impressionable. Suffering from low self-esteem, I thought that the Christians around me had mastered a level of holiness that seemed to evade me. They seemed so changed, so sure, and so stable! I earnestly prayed, "Make me better, Lord!"

I don't think I have changed that prayer, but I have changed the motivation behind it. I had always been surrounded by a love that was based upon performance. So I thought God's love was doled out according to a merit system. If I did well today, God loved me. However, if I failed, He did not love me. I didn't know whether I was accepted in the Beloved, or not! Suddenly, I began to realize that God loved me as I was, although I had never been taught about perfect love.

For all have sinned and fall short of the glory of God
(ROMANS 3:23).

———•◦•———

No one person needs any more of the blood of
Jesus than the other. Jesus died once and for all.
Humanity must come to God on equal terms, each
individual totally helpless to earn his or her way to
Him. When we come to Him with this attitude, He
raises us up by the blood of Christ. He doesn't raise us
up because we do good things. He raises us up because
we have faith in the finished work on the Cross.

Many in the Church were striving for holiness. We
were trying to perfect flesh. Flesh is in enmity against
God, whether we paint it or not.

What is holiness? To understand it, we must first
separate the pseudo from the genuine because, when
you come into a church, it is possible to walk away
feeling like a second-class citizen. Many start going
overboard trying to be a super spiritual person in
order to compensate for an embarrassing past. You
can't earn deliverance. You have to just receive it
by faith. Christ is the only righteousness that God
will accept.

And He said to me, "My grace is sufficient for you, for My strength is made perfect in weakness..." (2 CORINTHIANS 12:9).

———•○•———

When the AIDS epidemic hit this country, pandemonium erupted. Terror caused many people, Christians as well as non-Christians, to react out of ignorance and intimidation. People were whispering, wanting to know how it was contracted. In my church it is absolutely absurd to concern themselves with how anybody contracted AIDS. The issue is, they have it and what are we going to do to help.

If we intend to accomplish anything, we must react to adversity like yeast. Once yeast is thoroughly stirred into the dough, it cannot be detected. Although it is invisible, it is highly effective. When the heat is on, it will rise. The warmer the circumstance, the greater the reaction. Likewise, God sets us in warm, uncomfortable places so we can rise. Sometimes the worst times in our lives do more to strengthen us than all our mountaintop experiences. The power of God reacts to struggle and stress. Isn't that what God meant when He told Paul, *"...My strength is made perfect in weakness."*

All Scripture is given by inspiration of God, and is profitable for doctrine, for reproof, for correction, for instruction in righteousness, that the man of God may be complete, thoroughly equipped for every good work (2 TIMOTHY 3:16-17).

---·○·---

When I was saved, no one shared with me that they had experienced struggles before they obtained victories. No one told me that wars come before success.

I tried to measure up to others and answer all the concerns that plagued my heart. I felt ashamed. My heart cried out, "What must I do to be perfected in the Lord?"

It is important for us to let God mature us—without our self-help efforts to impress others with a false sense of piety. That kind of do-it-yourself righteousness and religion keeps us from being naked before God and from being comfortable with our own level of growth. Yes, I want to be all that God wants me to be. But while I am developing at the rate He has chosen, I will certainly thank Him for His rich grace and bountiful mercy along the way. This is the divine mercy that lets us mature naturally.

Therefore I make known to you that no one speaking by the Spirit of God calls Jesus accursed, and no one can say that Jesus is Lord except by the Holy Spirit (I CORINTHIANS 12:3).

———•◦•———

There is a sanctity of your spirit that comes through the blood of the Lord Jesus Christ and sanctifies the innermost part of your being. Certainly, once you get cleaned up in your spirit, it will be reflected in your character and conduct. The Spirit of the Lord will give you boundaries. People must be loosed from the chains of guilt and condemnation. Many women in particular have been bound by manipulative messages that specialize in control and dominance.

The Church must open its doors and allow people who have a past to enter in. The Bible never camouflaged the weaknesses of the people God used. God used David. God used Abraham. We must divorce our embarrassment about wounded people. Yes, we've got wounded people. Yes, we've got hurting people. Sometimes they break the boundaries and they become lascivious and out of control and we have to readmit them into the hospital and allow them to be treated again. That's what the Church is designed to do. The Church is a hospital for wounded souls.

Not only so, but we also glory in our sufferings, because we know that suffering produces perseverance; perseverance, character; and character, hope (ROMANS 5:3-4 NIV).

---•◦•---

Relentless is a word I use to describe people who will not take no for an answer! They try things one way, and if that doesn't work, they try it another way. But they don't give up. You who are about to break beneath the stress of intense struggles—be relentless! Do not quit!

A terrible thing happens to people who give up too easily. It is called regret. It is the nagging, gnawing feeling that says, "If I had tried harder, I could have succeeded." Granted, we all experience some degree of failure. That is how we learn and grow. The problem isn't failure; it is when we fail and question if it was our lack of commitment that allowed us to forfeit an opportunity to turn the test into a triumph! We can never be sure of the answer unless we rally our talents, muster our courage, and focus our strength to achieve a goal. If we don't have the passion to be relentless, then we should leave it alone.

But we have this treasure in earthen vessels, that the excellence of the power may be of God, and not of us (2 CORINTHIANS 4:7).

---◦•◦---

Many Christians struggle to produce a premature change when God-ordained change can only be accomplished according to His time. We cannot expect to change the flesh. It will not respond to therapy. God intends for us to grow spiritually while we live in our vile, corrupt flesh. While we are changed in our spirit by the new birth, our old corruptible body and fleshly desires are not. It is His will that our treasure be displayed in a cabinet of putrid, unregenerated flesh— openly displaying the strange dichotomy between the temporal and the eternal.

It is amazing that God would put so much in so little. The true wonder of His glory is painted on the dark canvas of our old personhood. What a glorious backdrop our weakness makes for His strength!

There is a great deal of power released through the friction of the holy graces of God grating against the dry, gritty surface of human incapacities and limitations. We sharpen our testimonies whenever we press His glory against our struggles.

[Jesus said] *"Come to Me, all you who labor and are heavy laden, and I will give you rest"* (MATTHEW 11:28).

---•◦•---

We have all wrestled with something, though it may not always be the same challenge. My struggle may not be yours. If I'm wrestling with something that's not a problem to you, you do not have the responsibility for judging me when all the while you are wrestling with something equally as incriminating.

Regardless of what a person has done, or what kind of abuse one has suffered, God still calls. Rest assured that He knows all about our secrets, and still draws us with an immutable call.

No matter how difficult life seems, people with a past need to make their way to Jesus. Regardless of the obstacles within and without, they must reach Him. You may have a baby out of wedlock cradled in your arms, but keep pressing on. You may have been abused and molested and never able to talk to anyone about it, but don't cease reaching out for Him. You don't have to tell everyone your entire history. He knows your history, but He called you anyway.

Even so you, since you are zealous for spiritual gifts, let it be for the edification of the church that you seek to excel (I CORINTHIANS 14:12).

---◦○◦---

You would be surprised to know how many people there are who never focus on a goal. They do several things haphazardly without examining how forceful they can be when they totally commit themselves to a cause. The difference between the masterful and the mediocre is often a focused effort. On the other hand, mediocrity is masterful to persons of limited resources and abilities. So in reality, true success is relative to ability. What is a miraculous occurrence for one person can be nothing of consequence to another. A person's goal must be set on the basis of his ability to cultivate talents and his agility in provoking a change.

I am convinced that I have not fully developed my giftings. I am committed to being all that I was intended and predestined to be for the Lord, for my family, and for myself. How about you—have you decided to roll up your sleeves and go to work? Remember, effort is the bridge between mediocrity and masterful accomplishment!

In whom the whole building, being fitted together, grows into a holy temple in the Lord, in whom you also are being built together for a dwelling place of God in the Spirit (EPHESIANS 2:21-22).

———•○•———

Within our decaying shells, we constantly peel away, by faith, the lusts and jealousies that adorn the walls of our hearts. If the angels were to stroll through the earth with the Creator and ask, "Which house is Yours?" He would pass by all the mansions and cathedrals, all the temples and castles. Unashamedly, He would point at you and me and say, "That house is Mine!"

Yes, it is true: Despite all our washing and painting, this old house is still falling apart! We train it and teach it. We desperately try to convince it to at least think differently. But like a squeaky hinge on a swollen door, the results of our efforts, at best, come slowly. The Holy Ghost Himself resides beneath this sagging roof.

God Himself has—of His own free will and predetermined purpose—put us in the embarrassing situation of entertaining a Guest whose lofty stature so far exceeds us that we hardly know how to serve Him!

As for me, I will call upon God, and the Lord shall save me. Evening and morning and at noon I will pray, and cry aloud, and He shall hear my voice. He has redeemed my soul in peace... (PSALM 55:16-18).

————•○•————

Jesus' actions were massively different from ours. He focused on helping hurting people. Every time He saw a hurting person, He reached out and ministered to their need. Once when He was preaching, He looked through the crowd and saw a man with a withered hand. He immediately healed him (see Mark 3:1-5). He sat with the prostitutes and the winebibbers, not the upper echelon of His community. Jesus surrounded Himself with broken, bleeding, dirty people. He called a woman who was crippled and bent over (see Luke 13:11-13). She had come to church and sat in the synagogue for years and years and nobody had helped that woman until Jesus saw her. He called her to the forefront.

Why didn't He speak the word and heal her in her seat? Perhaps God wants to see us moving toward Him. We need to invest in our own deliverance. We will bring a testimony out of a test.

But I discipline my body and bring it into subjection, lest, when I have preached to others, I myself should become disqualified (I CORINTHIANS 9:27).

---•◦•---

Our struggle is to continuously feed the ravenous appetite of the Holy Spirit. He daily consumes, and continually requires, that which we alone know God wants from us. Paul battled to bring into submission the hidden things in his life that could bring destruction. Perhaps they were putrid thoughts, or vain imaginations, or pride; but whatever they were, he declared war on them if they resisted change. He says, in essence, that as he waits for the change, he keeps his body in chains, beating back the forces of evil.

This is the struggle of the same man who wrote the majority of the New Testament! With a testimony like this, I pay very little attention to those among us who feel obligated to impress us with the ludicrous idea that they have already attained what is meant to be a lifelong pursuit. The renewal of the old man is a daily exercise of the heart. It progressively strengthens the character day by day, not overnight!

He has delivered us from the power of darkness and conveyed us into the kingdom of the Son of His love (COLOSSIANS 1:13).

⎯⎯⎯●○●⎯⎯⎯

Many of the people who were a part of the ministry of Jesus' earthly life were people with colorful pasts. Some had indeed always looked for the Messiah to come. Others were involved in things that were immoral and inappropriate.

A good example is Matthew. He was a man who worked in an extremely distasteful profession. He was a tax collector. Few people like tax collectors still today. Their reputation was even worse at that time in history. Matthew collected taxes for the Roman empire. He had to have been considered a traitor by those who were faithful Jews. Romans were their oppressors. How could he have forsaken his heritage and joined the Romans? Regardless of his past, Jesus called Matthew to be a disciple. We must maintain a strong line of demarcation between a person's past and present.

These were the people Jesus wanted to reach. He was criticized for being around questionable characters. Everywhere He went the oppressed and the rejected followed Him. They knew that He offered mercy and forgiveness.

Who has saved us and called us with a holy calling, not according to our works, but according to His own purpose and grace which was given to us in Christ Jesus before time began (2 TIMOTHY 1:9).

⸻◦⸻

If you are only talented, you may feel comfortable taking your talents into a secular arena. Talent, like justice, is blind; it will seek all opportunities the same. But when you are cognizant of divine purpose, there are some things you will not do because they would defeat the purpose of God in your life! Being called according to purpose enables you to focus on the development of your talent as it relates to your purpose!

Whenever we bring our efforts into alignment with His purpose, we automatically are blessed. Our efforts must be tailored after the pattern of divine purpose. Everyone is already blessed. We often spend hours in prayer trying to convince God that He should bless what we are trying to accomplish. What we need to do is spend hours in prayer for God to reveal His purpose. When we do what God has ordained to be done, we are blessed because God's plan is already blessed.

> *For we know that if the earthly tent we live in is destroyed, we have a building from God, an eternal house in heaven, not built by human hands.... God... has given us the Spirit as a deposit, guaranteeing what is to come* (2 CORINTHIANS 5:1,5 NIV).

———•○•———

S o the bad news is that the old house is still a death trap; it's still infested with rodents. A legion of thoughts and pesky memories crawl around in our heads like roaches that come out in the night and boldly parade around the house. That should not negate our joy, though; it merely confesses our struggles.

The Guest we entertain desires more for us than what we have in us! He enjoys neither the house nor the clothing we offer Him. Jesus said, *"...every city or house divided against itself shall not stand"* (Matt. 12:25). Ever since we were saved, there has been a division in the house. Eventually the old house will have to yield to the new one! Yes, we are constantly renovating through the Word of God, but the truth is that God will eventually recycle what you and I have been trying to renovate!

For in my inner being I delight in God's law; but I see another law at work in me, waging war against the law of my mind and making me a prisoner of the law of sin at work within me (ROMANS 7:22-23 NIV).

————•◦•————

Christianity means conflict. At the least, if it doesn't mean conflict, it certainly creates conflict! Living holy isn't natural. It isn't natural—it is spiritual! Unless we walk consistently in the Spirit, living holy is difficult. No, it is impossible!

Without God it cannot be done! Being a Christian means that one part of you is constantly wanting to do the right thing while the other part of you is desperately campaigning for you to walk in your old habits. After I was saved, I didn't commit those wicked sins, but I would have had He not set up a protest in my heart! He brought my trembling soul to His bleeding side and cleansed my very imaginations, intentions, and ambitions! Yes, the Christian life is a life of conflict, and I thank God that He groans and protests my sinful behavior. It is because He challenges my proclivities that growth begins!

Stand fast therefore in the liberty liberty by which Christ has made us free, and be not entangled again with the yoke of bondage (GALATIANS 5:1).

---•◦•---

When Christ taught in the temple courts, there were those who tried to trap Him in His words. They knew that His ministry appealed to the masses of lowly people. They thought that if they could get Him to say some condemning things, the people wouldn't follow Him anymore.

The blood of Jesus is efficacious, cleansing the woman who feels unclean. How can we reject what He has cleansed and made whole? Just as He said to the woman then, He proclaims today, *"Neither do I condemn you; go and sin no more"* (John 8:11). How can the Church do any less?

The chains that bind are often from events that we have no control over. Other times the chains are there because we have willfully lived lives that bring bondage and pain.

Regardless of the source, Jesus comes to set us free. He is unleashing the persecuted of His Church. He forgives, heals, and restores. Believers can find the potential of their future because of His wonderful power operating in their lives.

Lord, how many are my foes! ...But you, Lord, are a shield around me, my glory, the One who lifts my head high. I call out to the Lord, and he answers me from his holy mountain (PSALM 3:1-4 NIV).

---·•◦•·---

David declares that it is the Lord who sustains you in the perilous times of inner struggle and warfare. It is the precious peace of God that eases your tension when you are trying to make decisions in the face of criticism and cynicism. When you realize that some people do not want you to be successful, the pressure mounts drastically. Many have said, "God will not deliver him." However, many saying it still doesn't make it true. I believe that the safest place in the whole world is in the will of God. If you align your plan with His purpose, success is imminent! On the other hand, if I have not been as successful as I would like to be, then seeking the purpose of God inevitably enriches my resources and makes the impossible attainable.

If the storm comes and I know I am in the will of God, then little else matters.

Against You, You only, have I sinned, and done this evil in Your sight—that You may be found just when You speak, and blameless when You judge (PSALM 51:4).

⸻⸻•○•⸻⸻

S aul was anointed by God to be king. He was more moral than David in that he didn't struggle in some of the areas that plagued David. His weakness wasn't outward; it was inward. Saul looked like a king, whereas David looked like an underage juvenile delinquent who should have been home taking care of the flocks. Saul's armor shined in the noonday sun. David had no armor. Even his weapon looked substandard; it was just an old, ragged, shepherd's slingshot.

Although David's weapon was outwardly substandard, it was nevertheless lethal; it led to the destruction of the giant. We can never destroy our enemy with the superficial armor of a pious king. We don't need the superficial. We need the supernatural! David's naked, transparent demeanor was so translucent that he often seems extremely vulnerable. You would almost think he was unfit, except that when he repents, there is something so powerful in his prayer that even his most adamant critic must admire his openness with God!

Then the scribes and Pharisees brought to Him a woman caught in adultery. And when they had set her in the midst, they said to Him, "Teacher, this woman was caught l in adultery, in the very act. ...So when they continued asking Him, He raised Himself up and said to them, "He who is without sin among you, let him throw a stone at her first" (JOHN 8:3-4,7).

---••◦••---

Clearly Jesus saw the foolish religious pride in their hearts. He was not condoning the sin of adultery. He simply understood the need to meet people where they were and minister to their need. He saw the pride in the Pharisees and ministered correction to that pride. He saw the wounded woman and ministered forgiveness. Justice demanded that she be stoned to death. Mercy threw the case out of court. Jesus, however, knew the power of a second chance.

There are those today who are very much like this woman. They have come into the Church. They have been stoned and ridiculed. They may not be physically broken and bowed over, but they are wounded within. Somehow the Church must find room to throw off condemnation and give life and healing.

> *Then Saul said to Samuel, "I have sinned, for I have transgressed the commandment of the Lord and your words, because I feared the people and obeyed their voice"* (I SAMUEL 15:24).

———•○•———

What a sharp contrast there is between David and King Saul, whose stately demeanor and pompous gait didn't stop him from being an incredible deceiver. Even when face to face with Samuel the prophet, Saul lied at a time he should have repented! The problem with people like Saul is that they are more interested in their image than they are concerned about being immaculate in their hearts.

While Saul stood arrayed in his kingly attire, boasting of his conquest over an enemy king and lying about his real struggles, the heathen king whom Saul had been commanded to kill was still alive. The sheep that he had been ordered to destroy were still bleating in the valley. God did not destroy Saul for not killing what he should have killed; that wasn't the biggest problem. The central problem was that Saul's deceitfulness had become a breach too wide to bridge. David might have been weak and struggled with moral issues, but at least he was naked before God!

As one whom his mother comforts, so will I comfort you; and you shall be comforted in Jerusalem (ISAIAH 66:13).

———•◦•———

I remember when our car broke down. It didn't have too far to break down because it already was at death's door. At the time, though, I needed to get uptown to ask the electric company not to cut off the only utility I had left. I pleaded with them but they cut it off anyway. I was crushed. I had been laid off my job, and my church was so poor it couldn't even pay attention. I walked out of the utility off ice and burst into tears. I looked like an insane person walking down the street. I was at the end of my rope.

To this melodramatic outburst God said absolutely nothing. He waited until I had gained some slight level of composure and then spoke. He said, *"I will not allow your foot to be moved!"* (See Psalm 121:3.) I shall never forget as long as I live the peace of His promise that came into my spirit. Suddenly the light, the gas, and the money didn't matter. What mattered was I knew I was not alone.

He who works deceit shall not dwell within my house; he who tells lies shall not continue in my presence (PSALM 101:7).

———•○•———

S aul had a terrible character flaw, that of deceit. Even when he was face to face with Samuel the prophet, Saul lied when he should have repented! (See First Samuel 15:15-24.) Saul represents that part of all of us that must be overthrown. We must renounce deceit if we are to go beyond the superficial and fulfill our destiny in the supernatural. There must be an open confession that enables God's grace to be allocated to your need.

There is a gradual transference of authority as we walk with God. We move from the Saul-like rule of superficial religion to a Davidic anointing based on honesty and transparency.

Only God knows the process it will take for Christ to be formed in you. He is taking each of us to that place where the child begins to bear a greater resemblance to his Father. Be assured that this only occurs at the end of travailing prayer and openness of heart, as we confess and forsake every trace of Saul's rule in our lives.

*You know my reproach, my shame, and my dishonor;
my adversaries are all before You* (PSALM 69:19).

———◦———

Israel was at its zenith under the leadership of a godly
king named David. There can be no argument that
David frequently allowed his passions to lead him into
moral failure. However, he was a man who recognized
his failures and repented. He was a man who sought
God's heart.

Although David longed to follow God, some of
his passions and lust were inherited by his children.
Maybe they learned negative things from their father's
failures. That is a tendency we must resist. We ought
not repeat the failure of our fathers. We are most vulnerable, however, to our father's weaknesses. David's
son, Amnon, demonstrated one of these weaknesses
as he shamed his half sister, Tamar, by raping her.

The name Tamar means "palm tree." Tamar is
a survivor. She still stands. When the cold blight of
winter stands up in her face, she withstands the chilly
winds and remains green throughout the winter.
Tamar is a survivor. You are a survivor. Through hard
times God has granted you the tenacity to endure
stresses and strains.

He delivered me from my strong enemy, from those who hated me, for they were too strong for me. They confronted me in the day of my calamity, but the Lord was my support (PSALM 18:17-18).

---◦•◦---

There is a deep-seated need in all of us to sense purpose—even out of calamity. Out of this thirst for meaning is born the simplistic yet crucial prayer, "Why?"

No matter how painful the quest, we will still search through the rubbish of broken dreams, broken promises, and twisted childhood issues looking for clues. We don't have to necessarily erase the cause of our pain; we mainly just want to find some reason or justification for the pain and discomfort.

All of us know what it means to be left alone. Whether through death, desertion, or even disagreement, we have all been left alone at times. We are sometimes disillusioned when we find out how easily people will leave us. Generally they leave us when we think that we need them.

The struggle truly begins not when people surround us, but rather when they forsake us. It is then that we begin to discover our own identity and self-worth!

For who has despised the day of small things? For these seven rejoice to see the plumb line in the hand... (ZECHARIAH 4:10).

———•◦•———

I remember so well the early struggles that my wife and I had to maintain our family, finances, and overall well-being while building a ministry. I was working a secular job that God wanted me to leave for full-time ministry. Full-time ministry—what a joke! I was scarcely asked to preach anywhere that offered more than some food. Often I would preach until sweaty and tired, to rows of empty pews with two or three people who decorated the otherwise empty church.

Finally I said yes to full-time ministry. I did it not because I wanted it, but because the company I worked for went out of business and I was forced out of my comfort zone into the land of faith. What a frightening experience. I was without everything you could think of: without a job and then a car. I thought God had forgotten me. But I experienced more about God in those desperate days of struggle as I answered the charges of satan with the perseverance of prayer.

It is good for me that I have been afflicted; that I may learn Your statutes (PSALM 119:71).

———•○•———

What happens when friendship takes an unusual form? Did you know that God, our ultimate Friend, sometimes manipulates the actions of our enemies to cause them to work as friends in order to accomplish His will in our lives? God can bless you through the worst of relationships! That is why we must learn how to accept even the relationships that seem to be painful or negative. The time, effort, and pain we invest in them is not wasted because God knows how to make adversity feed destiny into your life!

I cannot stop your hurts from coming; neither can I promise that everyone who sits at the table with you is loyal. But I can suggest that the sufferings of success give us direction and build character within us. Finally, you find the grace to reevaluate your enemies and realize that many of them were friends in disguise. As God heals what hurts you have, remember that betrayal is only sweetened when it is accompanied by survival. Live on, my friend, live on!

Therefore we do not lose heart. Though outwardly we are wasting away, yet inwardly we are being renewed day by day. For our light and momentary troubles are achieving for us an eternal glory that far outweighs them all (2 CORINTHIANS 4:16-17 NIV).

———•◦•———

We went through a phase once when we thought real faith meant having no feelings. Although we don't want to be controlled by feelings, we must have access to our emotions. We need to allow ourselves the pleasure and pain of life.

Emotional pain is to the spirit what physical pain is to the body. Pain warns us that something is out of order and may require attention. Pain warns us that something in our body is not healed. When pain fills our heart, we know that we have an area where healing or restoration is needed. We dare not ignore these signals, and neither dare we let them control us.

We need to allow the Spirit of God to counsel us and guide us through the challenges of realignment when upheavals occur in our lives. Even the finest limousine requires a regular schedule of tune-ups or realignments. Minor adjustments increase performance and productivity.

You let people ride over our heads; we went through fire and water, but you brought us to a place of abundance (PSALM 66:12 NIV).

———•○•———

S atan cannot dispute your serving God, but he challenges our reason for serving Him. He says it is for the prominence and protection that God provides. He insinuates that if things weren't going so well, we would not praise God so fervently. In each of our lives, in one way or another, we will face times when we must answer satan's charges and prove that even in the storm, He is still God!

Times of challenge in my early ministry sorely tried all that was in me. If you can remember your beginnings and still reach toward your goals, God will bless you with things without fear of those items becoming idols in your life. There is a glory in the early years that people who didn't have to struggle seem not to possess. There is a strange sense of competence that comes from being born in the flames of struggle. How exuberant are the first steps of the child who earlier was mobile only through crawling on his hands and knees.

Rescue the weak and the needy; deliver them from the hand of the wicked (PSALM 82:4 NIV).

———◦———

The enemy wants to violate God's children. He is planning and plotting your destruction. He has watched you with wanton eyes. He has great passion and perseverance. Jesus told Peter, *"...Satan has asked to sift all of you as wheat. But I have prayed for you..."* (Luke 22:31-32 NIV). Satan lusts after God's children. He wants you. He craves for you with an animalistic passion. He awaits an opportunity for attack. In addition, he loves to use people to fulfill the same kinds of lust upon one another.

Often the residual effects of being abused linger for many years. Some never find deliverance because they never allow Christ to come into the dark places of their life. Jesus has promised to set you free from every curse of the past. He wants the whole person well—in body, emotions, and spirit. He will deliver you from all the residue of your past. Perhaps the incident is over but the crippling is still there. He also will deal with the crippling that's left in your life.

Consider it pure joy, my brothers and sisters, whenever you face trials of many kinds, because you know that the testing of your faith produces perseverance (JAMES 1:2-3 NIV).

———•○•———

In spite of the pain and distaste of adversity, it is impossible not to notice that each adverse event leaves sweet nectar behind, which, in turn, can produce its own rich honey in the character of the survivor. It is this bittersweet honey that allows us to enrich the lives of others through our experiences and testimonies. There is absolutely no substitute for the syrupy nectar of human experiences. It is these experiences that season the future relationships God has in store for us.

Unfortunately, many people leave their situation bitter and not better. Be careful to bring the richness of the experience to the hurting, not the unresolved bitterness. This kind of bitterness is a sign that the healing process in you is not over and, therefore, is not ready to be shared. You must come to a place of separation and decide to live on. When we have gone through the full cycle of survival, the situations and experiences in our lives will produce no pain, only peace.

DAY 64

Therefore thus says the Lord God: "Behold, I lay in Zion a stone for a foundation, a tried stone, a precious cornerstone, a sure foundation; whoever believes will not act hastily" (ISAIAH 28:16).

———•◦•———

I have found God to be a builder. When He builds, He emphasizes the foundation. A foundation, once it is laid, is neither visible nor attractive, but nevertheless still quite necessary. When God begins to establish the foundation, He does it in the feeble, frail beginnings of our lives. Paul describes himself as a wise master builder. Actually, God is the Master Builder. He knows what kind of beginning we need and He lays His foundation in the struggles of our formative years.

I don't think I completely realized how severe my early years of ministry were because I saw them through the tinted glasses of grace. I had been gifted with the grace to endure. Often we don't realize how severe our beginnings were until we are out or about to come out of them. Then the grace lifts and we behold the utter devastating truth about what we just came through.

The Lord possessed me in the beginning of His way, before His works of old....Then I was by Him, as one brought up with Him: and I was daily His delight, rejoicing always before Him. (PROVERBS 8:22,30 KJV).

———•○•———

The streaming fount of holy blood that flows from the gaping wounds of my loving Savior has draped my wretchedness in His holiness. He has covered me like Boaz covered Ruth. His blood also has covered me like a warm blanket on a cold night. I found my past nestled beneath His omnipresent banner of love and concern, taking the chill out of my life and removing the stiffness from my heart. When I had no one to snuggle close to, He became my eternal companion— always seeking out what is best for me and bringing before me great and mighty things

I confess that I often used to resist loneliness. I filled my life with work and with people who meant me no good at all. At that time, I would rather have filled my life with noise than run the risk of total silence. How foolish of me not to note the difference between being alone and being lonely.

Then He arose and rebuked the wind, and said to the sea, "Peace, be still!" And the wind ceased and there was a great calm (MARK 4:39).

———•◦•———

Have you allowed God to stand in the bow of your ship and speak peace to the thing that once terrified you? We can only benefit from resolved issues. The great tragedy is that most of us keep our pain active. Our power is never activated because our past remains unresolved. If we want to see God's power come from the pain of an experience, we must allow the process of healing to take us beyond bitterness into a resolution that releases us from the prison and sets us free.

To never trust again is to live on the pinnacle of a tower. You always talk about the past because you stopped living years ago. Listen to your speech. You discuss the past as if it were the present because the past has stolen the present right out of your hand! In the name of Jesus, get it back! God's healing process makes us free to taste life again, free to trust again, and free to live without threatening fears.

Brothers and sisters, I could not address you as people who live by the Spirit but as people who are still worldly—mere infants in Christ (I CORINTHIANS 3:I NIV).

———•◦•———

When I was very small, my family had a tradition we observed every Sunday breakfast. Every Sunday morning my mother would go into the kitchen while we were still asleep and begin making homemade waffles for breakfast. These were real waffles. I don't remember all the ingredients she had in them, but I do remember that this particular recipe required beating the egg whites and then folding them into the waffle batter.

They smelled like Hallelujah and they looked like glory to God—if you know what I mean. They took a long time to prepare, but these waffles took your mouth to the butter-filled streams of heaven.

The other day I tasted some of these modern carbon copy, freezer burned, cardboard-clad waffles. My taste buds recoiled. My point is, I am afraid that too many Christians pop off the altar like these cardboard waffles. They are overnight wonders. They are 24-hour pastors with a Bible they haven't read and a briefcase more valuable than the sermons in it!

Now also when I am old and greyheaded, O God, do not forsake me; until I declare Your strength to this generation, and Your power to every one who is to come (PSALM 71:18).

─────◦○◦─────

I recently had the privilege of entertaining my 90-yearold grandmother, whose robust frame has deteriorated to just a mere shadow of its former presence.

This was the Trojan-like woman who had worked her way through college doing laundry, studying in the wee hours of the night. This was the Mississippi matron who captured a teaching degree in the middle of her life. Now she had come to the setting of the sun.

I could see that sun burning behind her leathery skin and glazed eyes. Age had somehow smothered her need to talk, and she would lapse into long periods of silence that left me clamoring foolishly through asinine conversations. Whenever I asked her if she was all right, she would respond affirmatively and assure me that she was greatly enjoying my company. Then she would flee into the counsel of her own thoughts and come out at intervals to play with me, with some humorous statement that would remind me of her earlier years.

Be still, and know that I am God: I will be exalted among the nations, I will be exalted in the earth!
(PSALM 46:10)

———•◦•———

All too often, our thoughts and conversations reveal that we wrestle with characters who have moved on and events that don't really matter. The people who surround us are kept on hold while we invest massive amounts of attention to areas of the past that are dead and possess no ability to reward.

I think that the greatest of all depressions comes when we live and gather our successes just to prove something to someone who isn't even looking. God did most of His work on creation with no one around to applaud His accomplishments. So He praised Himself. He said, "It was good!"

Have you stopped to appreciate what God has allowed you to accomplish, or have you been too busy trying to make an impression on someone? Somewhere beyond loneliness there is contentment, and contentment is born out of necessity. It springs up in the heart that lives in an empty house, and in the smile that comes on the face of a person who has amused himself with his own thoughts.

But, beloved, do not forget this one thing, that with the Lord one day is as a thousand years, and a thousand years as one day (2 PETER 3:8).

———•◦•———

God takes His time developing us. A small beginning is just the prelude to a tremendous crescendo at the finale! Many of God's masterpieces were developed in small obscure circumstances. Moses, sent to the lost sheep of Israel, was trained in leadership while shoveling sheep dung on the backside of the desert. Granted, his discipline was developed in the royal courts of Pharaoh's house, but his disposition was shaped through failure and a desert kingdom with no one to lead but flies, gnats, and sheep. Who would have thought, looking at Moses' church of goat deacons and gnats for choir members, that he later would lead the greatest movement in the history of Old Testament theology?

You can't tell what's in you by looking at you. God is establishing patience, character, and concentration in the school of "nothing seems to be happening." Just because God promises to move in your life and anoints you to do a particular function doesn't mean that your foundation will be immediately built.

Behold, I go forward, but He is not there; and backward, but I cannot perceive Him: on the left hand, where He doth work, but I cannot behold, Him; He hideth Himself on the right hand, that I cannot see Him (JOB 23:8-9 KJV).

———•◦•———

There are times when it is difficult to understand God's methods. There are moments when discerning His will is frustrating. Perhaps we have these moments because we haven't been given all the information we need to ascertain His ways as well as His acts. Many times we learn more in retrospect than we do while in the thick of the struggle. I can look at my past and see that the hand of the Lord has been on me all my life. Yet there were times when I felt completely alone and afraid. Even Jesus once cried out, *"Eli, Eli, lama sabachthani? that is to say, My God, My God, why hast Thou forsaken Me?"* (Matt. 27:46) Suspended on the Cross with a bloody, beaten body, He was questioning the acts of God—but He never questioned His relationship with Him. Jesus says in essence, "I don't understand why, but You are still My God!"

In Him also we have obtained an inheritance, being predestined according to the purpose of Him who works all things according to the counsel of His will (EPHESIANS 1:11).

———◦◦◦———

Have you reached that place in life where you enjoy your own company? Have you taken the time to enjoy your own personhood? When other people give affirmation, it reflects their opinion about you. When they leave, you may feel worthless and insignificant. But when you speak comfort and blessings to yourself, it reflects your own opinion about yourself. The best scenario is to enjoy both kinds of affirmation.

There are reasons to give yourself a standing ovation. The first is the fact that your steps are carefully observed and arranged by God Himself. They are designed to achieve a special purpose in your life. The Bible says, *"If God is for us, who can be against us?"* (Rom. 8:31). So you must rejoice because you are in step with the beat of Heaven and the purposes of God. Second, you ought to rejoice because you are pursuing a goal that defies human manipulation. Your blessing rests in accomplishing the will of God.

Until we all reach unity in the faith and in the knowledge of the Son of God and become mature, attaining to the whole measure of the fullness of Christ (EPHESIANS 4:13 NIV).

———•○•———

Many misunderstand the prophecies of the Lord and so feel discontentment and despair. Just because God promises to move in your life and anoints you to do a particular function doesn't mean that your foundation will be immediately built. Joseph received a dream from the Lord that showed him ruling and reigning over his brothers, but in the next event his brothers stripped him, beat him, and tossed him in a hole...a dark hole of small beginnings.

Don't die in the hole! God hasn't changed His mind. He is a Master Builder and He spends extra time laying a great foundation.

When the first man Adam was created, he was created full grown. He had no childhood, no small things. But when it was time for the last man Adam, God didn't create Him full grown. No, He took His time and laid a foundation. He was born a child and laid in a manger. Please allow yourself time to grow.

*In the same way, let your light shine before others,
that they may see your good deeds and glorify your
Father in heaven* (MATTHEW 5:16 NIV).

———•◦•———

It is wonderful to have a plan, but that means nothing
if you have no power to perform the plan and accomplish the purpose. God sends people in and out of your
life to exercise your faith and develop your character.
When they are gone, they leave you with the reality
that your God is with you to deliver you wherever you
go! Moses died and left Joshua in charge, but God told
him, *"As I was with Moses, so I will be with you"* (Josh.
1:5). Joshua never would have learned that while Moses
was there. You learn this kind of thing when "Moses"
is gone. Power is developed in the absence of human
assistance. Then we can test the limits of our resourcefulness and the magnitude of the favor of God.

There is within the most timid person—beneath
that soft, flaccid demeanor—a God-given strength
that supercedes any weakness he appeared to have.
The Bible puts it this way: *"I can do all things through
Christ whho strengthens me"* (Phil. 4:13)!

The human spirit is the lamp of the Lord, that sheds light on one's inmost being (PROVERBS 20:27 NIV).

———◦———

As I pondered my 90-year-old grandmother's behavior and her silent, Indian-like demeanor, I realized that her silence was not boredom. It was, first of all, the mark of someone who has learned how to be alone. It reflected the hours she had spent sitting in a rocking chair, entertaining herself with her own thoughts, and reconciling old accounts that brought the past into balance before the books were presented to the Master Himself. She was at peace, with the kind of peace that comes from a firm faith and deep resolution.

I am rewarded with a friendly reminder from a loving God who speaks through the glazed eyes of an aged relative, telling me to relax and enjoy life. It was there that I made two commitments in my own mind, as my grandmother smiled and gazed out of a window as if she were looking at Heaven itself. I committed to a renewed faith and trust in the ableness of God. The other commitment I made may seem strange, but I promised to spend more time with myself, to warm myself at the fire of my own thoughts and smile with the contentments of the riches contained therein.

For even Christ did not please Himself; but as it is written, "The reproaches of those who reproached You fell on Me" (ROMANS 15:3).

———•○•———

Buried deep within the broken heart is a vital need to release and resolve. Although we feel pain when we fail at any task, there is a sweet resolve that delivers us from the cold clutches of uncertainty. If we had not been through some degree of rejection, we would have never been selected by God. Do you realize that God chooses people that others reject?! From a rejected son like David to a nearly murdered son like Joseph, God gathers the castaways of men and recycles them for Kingdom building.

What frustration exists in the lives of people who want to be used of God, but who cannot endure rejection from men. I haven't always possessed the personality profile that calloused me and offered some protection from the backlash of public opinion. If you want to be tenacious, you must be able to walk in the light of God's selection rather than dwell in the darkness of people's rejection. These critics are usually just a part of God's purpose in your life.

...and the winds blew and beat on that house; and it fell. And great was its fall (MATTHEW 7:27).

⸺•◦•⸺

Once I was praying for the Lord to move mightily in my ministry. The Lord answered my prayer by saying, "You are concerned about building a ministry, but I am concerned about building a man." He gave a warning, which has echoed throughout my life. He said, "Woe unto the man whose ministry becomes bigger than he is!" Since then I have concerned myself with praying for the minister and not for the ministry. I realized that if the house outgrows the foundation, gradually the foundation will crack, the walls will collapse, and great will be the fall of it! No matter what you are trying to build, whether it is a business, a ministry, or a relationship, give it time to grow.

Humility is a necessity when you know that every accomplishment had to be the result of the wise Master Builder who knows when to do what. He knew when I needed friends. I trust Him more dearly and more nearly than I have ever trusted Him before. He is too wise to make a mistake!

...The stone which the builders rejected has become the chief cornerstone. This was the Lord's doing, and it is marvelous in our eyes (MATTHEW 21:42).

———————•◦•———————

Jesus concluded that the rejections of men He experienced were the doings of the Lord! The Lord orchestrates what the enemy does and makes it accomplish His purpose in your life. If I hadn't faced trials, I wouldn't have been ready for the blessings I now enjoy.

In the hands of God, even our most painful circumstances become marvelous in our eyes! However, rejection is only marvelous in the eyes of someone whose heart has wholly trusted in the Lord! Do you trust in the Lord, or are you grieving over something that someone has done—as though you have no God to direct it and no grace to correct it?

This question challenges the perspectives you have chosen to take for your life. "It is marvelous in our eyes" simply means that from our perspective, the worst things look good!

Faith is not needed just to remove problems; it is also needed to endure problems that seem immovable. Even if God didn't move it, He is able!

Bear one another's burdens, and so fulfill the law of Christ (GALATIANS 6:2).

———•○•———

Love embraces the totality of the other person. It is impossible to completely and effectively love someone without being included in that other person's history. Our history has made us who we are. The images, scars, and victories that we live with have shaped us into the people we have become. We will never know who a person is until we understand where they have been.

The secret of being transformed from a vulnerable victim to a victorious, loving person is found in the ability to open your past to someone responsible enough to share your weaknesses and pains. You don't have to keep reliving it. You can release it. We are all in this walk together, and therefore can build one another up and carry some of the load with which other believers are burdened.

There is hope for victims. There is no need to feel weak when one has Jesus Christ. His power is enough to bring about the kinds of changes that will set you free. He is calling, through the work of the Holy Spirit, for you to be set free.

But to those who do not believe, "The stone the builders rejected has become the cornerstone" (1 PETER 2:7 NIV).

————•◦•————

Normally, anytime there is a crash, there is an injury. In the same way, a crashing relationship affects everyone associated with it, whether it is in a corporate office, a ministry, or a family. What is important is the fact that we don't have to die in the crashes and collisions of life. We must learn to live life with a seat belt in place, even though it is annoying to wear. Similarly, we need spiritual and emotional seat belts as well. We don't need the kind that harness us in and make us live like a mannequin; rather, we need the kind that are invisible, but greatly appreciated in a crash.

Inner assurance is the seat belt that stops you from going through the roof when you are rejected. It is inner assurance that holds you in place. It is the assurance that God is in control and that what He has determined no one can disallow! Praise God, for He will use the cornerstone developed through rejections and failed relationships to perfect what He has prepared!

Not that I speak in regard to need, for I have learned in whatever state I am, to be content: I know how to be abased, and I know how to abound...
(PHILIPPIANS 4:11-12).

———•◦•———

If you are praying, "Lord, make me bigger," you are probably miserable, although prayerful. Did you know you can be prayerful and still be miserable? Anytime you use prayer to change God, who is perfect, instead of using prayer to change yourself, you are miserable. Instead, try praying this: "Lord, make me better." I admit that better is harder to measure and not as noticeable to the eye. But better will overcome bigger every time.

What a joy it is to be at peace with who you are and where you are in your life. I want to be better—to have a better character, better confidence, and a better attitude! The desire to be bigger will not allow you to rest, relax, or enjoy your blessing. The desire to be better, however, will afford you a barefoot stroll down a deserted beach. Thank God for the things that you know He brought you through. Thank God for small things.

Listen to counsel and receive instruction, that you may be wise in your latter days (PROVERBS 19:20).

———————•◦•———————

This morning when I rose, I watched the miracle of beginnings from the veranda of my hotel. Far to the east the sun crept up on stage as if it was trying to arrive without disturbing anyone. It peeked up over the ocean like the eye of a child around a corner as he stealthily plays peek-a-boo.

If I had not stayed perched on my window's edge, I would have misjudged the day. I would have thought that the morning or perhaps the sun-drenched afternoon was the most beautiful part of the day. But just before I turned in my ballot and cast my vote, the evening slipped up on the stage. I looked over in the distance as the sun began its descent. I noticed that the crescendo of the concert is always reserved for the closing. The sun had changed her sundress to an evening gown, full of color and grandeur. The grace of a closing day is far greater than the uncertainty of morning. The most beautiful part of a woman's life, is at the setting of the sun.

*For you know that we dealt with each of you as
a father deals with his own children, encouraging,
comforting and urging you to live lives worthy of
God, who calls you into his kingdom and glory*
(I THESSALONIANS 2:11-12 NIV).

———•○•———

Isn't it amazing how we can see so much potential in
others, yet find it difficult to unlock our own hidden treasure? Nurturing is the investment necessary to
stimulate the potential that we possess. Without nurturing, inner strengths may remain dormant. Therefore
it is crucial to our development that there be some
degree of nurturing the intrinsic resources we possess.

There is a difference in the emotional makeup of
a child who has had a substantial deposit of affection
and affirmation. Great affirmation occurs when someone invests into our personhood. Anyone will invest
in a sure success, but aren't we grateful when someone
supports us when we were somewhat of a risk?

Unfortunately, nothing brings luster to your
character and commitment to your heart like opposition does. The finished product is a result of the
fiery process. It creates someone who shines with the
kind of brilliancy that enables God to look down and
see Himself.

You were taught, with regard to your former way of life, to put off your old self, which is being corrupted by its deceitful desires; to be made new in the attitude of your minds; and to put on the new self, created to be like God in true righteousness and holiness (EPHESIANS 4:22-24 NIV).

———◦———

Today, many of us have things we need to be separated from or burdens we need lifted. We can function to a certain point under a load, but we can't function as effectively as we would if the thing was lifted off of us. Perhaps some of you right now have things that are burdening you down.

It is God's intention that we be set free from the loads we carry. Many people live in codependent relationships. Others are anesthetized to their problems because they have had them so long. Perhaps you have become so accustomed to having a problem that even when you get a chance to be delivered, you find it hard to let it go. Problems can become like a security blanket.

Before you get out of trouble, straighten out your attitude. Until your attitude is corrected, you can't be corrected.

"Am I only a God nearby," declares the Lord, *"and not a God far away? Who can hide in secret places so that I cannot see them?"* declares the Lord." *Do not I fill heaven and earth?"* declares the Lord (JEREMIAH 23:23-24 NIV).

———•◦•———

There is no tiptoeing around the presence of God with pristine daintiness—as if we could tiptoe softly enough not to awaken a God who never sleeps nor slumbers. We shuffle in His presence like children who were instructed not to disturb their Father, although God isn't sleepy and He doesn't have to go to work. He is alive and awake, and He is well.

It is the nature of a fallen man to hide from God. If you will remember, Adam also hid from God. How ridiculous it is for us to think that we can hide from Him! His intelligence supercedes our frail ability to be deceptive. When a man hides himself from God, he loses himself. What good is it to know where everything else is, if we cannot find ourselves? Our loss causes a desperation that produces sin and separation. We need to become transparent in the presence of the Lord.

Finally, brethren, whatsoever things are true, whatsoever things are honest, whatsoever things are just, whatsoever things are pure, whatsoever things are lovely, whatsoever things are of good report; if there be any virtue, and if there be any praise, think on these things (PHILIPPIANS 4:8 KJV).

———— ◆◦◆ ————

We must understand that modern medicine can heal many afflictions of the body, and can even treat the tumors that sometimes attach themselves to the brain, but only God Himself can heal the mind. Do you know that many times your thoughts need to be healed? Your thoughts are often the product of damaged emotions, traumatic events, and vicious opinions forced upon you by the bodacious personalities of domineering people who continually feel it necessary to express their opinions about you.

You do have control over your thoughts. You must choose what you are going to meditate upon. Choose carefully, though, for you will ultimately become whatever it is you meditate upon. The enemy knows this, so when he wants to destroy your morality, he doesn't start with an act; he starts with a thought. A thought is a seed that, if not aborted, will produce offspring somewhere in your life.

*For He is like a refiner's fire and like launderers'
soap* (MALACHI 3:2).

───•◦•───

God places His prize possessions in the fire. The
precious vessels that He draws the most brilliant
glory from often are exposed to the melting pot of distress. The bad news is, even those who live godly lives
will suffer persecution. The good news is, you might be
in the fire, but God controls the thermostat! He knows
how hot it needs to be to accomplish His purpose in
your life. I don't know anyone I would rather trust with
the thermostat than the God of all grace.

Every test has degrees. Some people have experienced similar distresses, but to varying degrees. God
knows the temperature that will burn away the impu-
rities from His purpose. He has had to fan the flames
to produce the effects that He wanted in my life. God
is serious about producing the change in us that will
glorify Him.

His hand has fanned the flames that were needed
to teach patience, prayer, and many other invaluable
lessons. We need His corrections. We don't enjoy
them, but we need them. He affirms our position in
Him by correcting and chastening us.

Trust in the Lord with all your heart, and lean not on your own understanding; in all your ways acknowledge Him, and He shall direct your paths (PROVERBS 3:5-6).

———◦———

Discouragement comes when people feel they have seen it all and most of it was really terrible! No matter what age you are, you have never seen it all. There are no graduations from the school of life other than death. No one knows how God will end His book, but He does tend to save the best for last. Israel didn't recognize Jesus because they were so used to seeing what they had already seen. God had sent dozens of prophets, and when He finally sends a king, they failed to recognize Him.

It is dangerous to assume that what you will see out of life will be similar to what you saw before. God has the strangest way of restoring purpose to your life. For Naomi, it was through a relationship she tried to dissuade. It is dangerous to keep sending people away. The very one you are trying to send away may have the key to restoring purpose and fulfillment to your life.

Let us therefore come boldly to the throne of grace, that we may obtain mercy, and find grace to help in time of need (HEBREWS 4:16).

———◦◦◦———

Why would Adam, a lost man, cover himself with leaves? Adam said, "I was afraid." Fear separated this son from his Father; fear caused him to conspire to deceive his only Solution. This fear was not reverence. It was desperation.

If Adam had only run toward instead of away from God, he could have been delivered! Why then do we continue to present a God who cannot be approached to a dying world? Many in the Christian family are still uncomfortable with their Heavenly Father. Some Christians do not feel accepted in the Beloved. They feel that their relationship with God is meritorious, but they are intimidated because of His holiness. His holiness exposes our flaws. Yet His grace allows us to approach Him—though we are not worthy—through the bloody skins soaked with Christ's blood.

Who else knows you like God does? If you hide from His perfect love, you will never be able to enjoy a relationship with your Heavenly Father and be comfortable enough to sit in His lap.

Let the words of my mouth, and the meditation of my heart, be acceptable in Thy sight, O Lord, my strength, and my redeemer (PSALM 19:14 KJV).

———•◦•———

You must quickly cast down an evil thought. "Push the remote control" before it drains away your commitment to excellence and leaves you crying in the valley of regret. The real temptation to entertain thoughts is in the privacy of the mind. Who will know what you really think? You can smile at people and never disclose your innermost thoughts.

I always laugh when I see people act as though they have conquered the battle with the mind. I've asked people in my services, "Which of you would be comfortable with having everything that comes to mind played on a television screen for all of your Christian friends to watch? Or which of you would like to have all our thoughts through the week played over the loudspeaker at church next Sunday?" I'm sure I don't have to tell you, they all put their hands down.

Our mind is a private battleground that can easily become a secret place for contamination, lust, fear, low self-esteem, and God only knows what else!

Most assuredly, I say to you, unless a grain of wheat falls into the ground and dies, it remains alone; but if it dies, it produces much grain (JOHN 12:24).

———◦———

I t is impossible to discuss the value of investing in people and not find ourselves worshiping God— what a perfect picture of investment. God is the major stockholder. No matter who He later uses to enhance our characters, we need to remember the magnitude of God's investment in our lives. The greatest primary investment He made was the inflated, unthinkable price of redemption that He paid. No one else would have bought us at that price. He paid the ultimate price when He died for our sins.

God has an investment in our lives. First of all, no one invests without the expectation of gain. What would a perfect God have to gain from investing in an imperfect man? According to Scripture, we possess treasure. However, the excellency of what we have is not of us, but of God. The treasure is "of" God. This treasure originates from God. It is accumulated in us and then presented back to Him. Your inheritance is encased in your treasure.

Therefore, since Christ suffered in his body, arm yourselves also with the same attitude, because he whoever suffers in the body is done with sin. As a result, they do not live the rest of their earthly lives for evil human desires, but rather for the will of God (1 PETER 4:1-2 NIV).

———•◦•———

Why should we put up all the ramps and rails for the handicapped if we can heal them? You want everyone to make an allowance for your problem, but your problem needs to make an allowance for God and to humble itself to the point where you don't need special help. I'm addressing the emotional baggage that keeps us from total health. You cannot expect the whole human race to move over because you had a bad childhood. They will not do it. You may have trouble with relationships because people don't accommodate your hang-up.

Christ wants to separate you from the source of your bitterness until it no longer gives you the kind of attitude that makes you a carrier of pain. Your attitude affects your situation—your attitude, not other people's attitude about you. Your attitude will give you life or death.

I will say of the Lord, "He is my refuge and my fortress: my God, in Him will I trust" (PSALM 91:2).

———•◦•———

The basis of any relationship must be trust. Trusting God with your successes isn't really a challenge. The real test of trust is to be able to share your secrets, your inner failures and fears. A mutual enhancement comes into a relationship where there is intimacy based on honesty.

We have nothing to fear, for our honesty with the Father doesn't reveal anything to Him that He doesn't already know! He knows of your failure before you fail. His knowledge is all-inclusive. He knows our thoughts even as we unconsciously gather them together to make sense in our own mind!

Once we know this, all our attempts at silence and secrecy seem juvenile and ridiculous. When we pray, and more importantly, when we commune with God, we must have the kind of confidence and assurance that neither requires nor allows deceit. His love is incomprehensible, because there is nothing with which we can compare it! What we must do is accept the riches of His grace and stand in the shade of His loving arms.

"For I will restore health to you and heal you of your wounds," says the Lord... (JEREMIAH 30:17).

---◦---

It takes patience to overcome the effects of years of use and abuse. If you are not committed to getting back what you once had, you could easily decide that the process is impossible. Nevertheless, I assure you it is not impossible. David, the psalmist, declares, *"He restores my soul"* (Ps. 23:3). The term "restoreth" is a process. Only God knows what it takes to remove the build-up that may exist in your life.

Prejudice is to prejudge. People, even believers, have often prejudged God. However, He isn't finished yet. Therefore, you are not off course. Trust Him to see you through days that may be different from the ones you encountered earlier. You are being challenged with the silent struggles of winter. I believe the most painful experience is to look backward and have to stare into the cold face of regret. First pause and thank God that, in spite of the tragedies of youth, it is a miracle that you survived the solemn chill of former days. Your presence should be a praise.

But He knows the way that I take; when He has tested me, I shall come forth as gold (JOB 23:10).

———•○•———

We spend most of our time talking about what we want from God. The real issue is what He wants from us. It is the Lord who has the greatest investment. We are the parched, dry ground from which Christ springs. Believe me, God is serious about His investment!

God will fight to protect the investment He has placed in your life. What a comfort it is to know that the Lord has a vested interest in my deliverance. God has begun the necessary process of cultivating what He has invested in my life. Have you ever stopped to think that it was God's divine purpose that kept you afloat when others capsized beneath the load of life? Look at Job; he knew that God had an investment in his life that no season of distress could eradicate.

Have you ever gone through a dilemma that should have scorched every area of your life and yet you survived the pressure? Then you ought to know that He is Lord over the fire!

You know my sitting down and my rising up; You understand my thought afar off (PSALM 139:2).

———•○•———

We shouldn't allow our minds to collect scum and clutter without any regard to cleaning and renewing the mind. Here are several reasons not to do that.

First, a certain Someone does know what we think. Second, we need to continually purge our thoughts because we become what we think. Third, we need to renew our minds daily in God's presence, for I believe that as we hear the thoughts of God, His thinking becomes increasingly contagious. Let's deal with the first of these three.

God sits in the living quarters of the minds of men and beholds their thoughts. He knows our thoughts afar off (see Ps. 139:2). If we are serious about entertaining His presence, we cannot lie to Him—He sees us from the inside out.

We must be honest and admit to Him: I know that if it were not for Your mercy, I would be guilty of the very things for which I have disdained others. I praise You for loving me, in spite of all You know about me.

Likewise the Spirit also helps in our weaknesses. For we do not know what we should pray for as we ought, but the Spirit Himself makes intercession for us with groanings which cannot be uttered (ROMANS 8:26).

⸺•◦•⸺

One thing we search for at every level of our relationships is "to be understood." When I am properly understood, I don't always have to express and explain. Thank You, Lord, for not asking me to explain what I oft can scarcely express!

We quickly grow weary when we are around anyone who demands that we constantly qualify our statements and explain our intent. But God clearly perceives and understands our every need.

We are to live in a state of open communication with God, not necessarily jabbering at Him nonstop for hours. Many people end up watching the clock while they utter mindless rhetoric, trying to get in the specified amount of time in prayer.

We don't need to labor to create what is already there. I am glad my Savior knows what my speech and my silence suggest. I need not labor to create what we already share in the secret place of our hearts!

...whatever you did for one of the least of these brothers and sisters of mine, you did for me (MATTHEW 25:40 NIV).

———•◦•———

Here is something every person can rely on during their winter season of life. The Lord will be known as: the nourisher. You, who have been the source for others to be strengthened, may find it difficult to know what to do with this role reversal. The nourisher must learn to be nourished. Many pray more earnestly as intercessors for others than for themselves. That is wonderful, but there ought to be a time that you desire certain things for yourself. Our God is El Shaddai, giving strength to the feeble and warmth to the cold. There is comfort in His arms. Like children, even adults can snuggle into His everlasting arms and hear the heartbeat of a loving God.

Expect God in all His varied forms. He is a master of disguise, a guiding star in the night, a lily left growing in the valley, or an answered prayer sent on the breath of an angel. God can use anyone as a channel of nourishment. Regardless of the channel, He is still the source.

When you pass through the waters, I will be with you; and through the rivers, they shall not overflow you. When you walk through the fire, you shall not be burned, nor shall the flame scorch you (ISAIAH 43:2).

---◦---

I t has been suggested that if you walk in the Spirit, you won't have to contend with the fire. Real faith doesn't mean you won't go through the fire. The presence of the Lord can turn a burning inferno into a walk in the park! The Bible says a fourth person was in the fire, and the three Hebrews were able to walk around unharmed in it (see Dan. 3).

King Nebuchadnezzar was astonished when he saw them overcome what had destroyed other men. I cannot guarantee that you will not face terrifying situations if you believe God. I can declare that if you face them with Christ's presence, the effects of the circumstance will be drastically altered. If you believe God, you can walk in what other people burn in. Seldom will anyone fully appreciate the fire you have walked through, but God knows the fiery path to accomplishment. He can heal the blistered feet of the traveler.

But without faith it is impossible to please Him, for he that comes to God must believe that He is, and that He is a rewarder of them that diligently seek Him (HEBREWS 11:6).

There are no manuals that instruct us step by step as to the proper way to seek the Lord. There are no rules—just that we seek Him with our whole hearts.

My friend, don't be afraid to stretch out your hands to reach after Him. Cry after Him. Whatever you do, do not allow this moment to pass you by!

Like groping fingers extended in the night trying to compensate for a darkened vision, we feel after God. We feel after His will and His ways. I'm amazed at all the people who seem to always know everything God is saying about everything. In their hymn, Ray Palmer and Lowell Mason wrote, "My faith looks up to thee, Oh lamb of Calvary, Savior divine." My faith looks up because my eyes can't always see. On the other hand, there is a healthy reaction that occurs in blindness; our senses become keener as we exercise areas that we wouldn't normally need.

And there is no creature hidden from His sight, but all things are naked and open to the eyes of Him to whom we must give account (HEBREWS 4:13).

———•◦•———

We are called to live in a state of openhearted communication with the Lord. Yes, we feel vulnerable when we realize that our hearts are completely exposed before God. Yet every one of us desperately needs to have someone who is able to help us, someone who is able to understand the issues that are etched on the tablets of our heart!

Since we already feel exposed when we realize that there is not one thought we have entertained that God has not seen and heard, then there is no need for a sanctimonious misrepresentation of who we are! We no longer need to live under the strain of continual camouflage. We are naked before Him, just as a man sprawls naked on the operating table before a surgeon. The man is neither boastful nor embarrassed, for he understands that his exposed condition is a necessity. We need to show God what is hindering His flow of life to us so He can clean us.

Being confident of this very thing, that He who has begun a good work in you will complete it until the day of Jesus Christ (PHILIPPIANS 1:6).

———•◦•———

I think it would be remiss of me not to share, before moving on, the miracles of winter. In the summer, all was well with Sarah. At that time she knew little about Jehovah, her husband's God. She basically knew she was in love with a wonderful man.

Soon the giddy exuberance of summer started to ebb as she began wrestling with the harsh realities of following a dreamer. What was really troubling her was the absence of a child. By now she was sure she was barren. She felt like she had cheated Abraham out of an important part of life. Someone had said she would have a baby. Sarah laughed, "If I am going to get a miracle, God had better hurry." I want to warn you against setting your own watch. God's time is not your time. He may not come when you want Him to, but He is right on time. After she had gone through life's experiences, she learned that God is faithful to perform His Word.

When you walk through the fire, you shall not be burned, nor shall the flame scorch you (ISAIAH 43:2).

———•◦•———

Your Deliverer knows what it feels like to be in the fire. Thank God for running swiftly to meet His children in the fire of affliction and need. But still the question remains, "Is there any preventive protection that will at least aid the victim who struggles in the throes of a fiery test?" If you are in a fiery trial, be advised that it is your faith that is on trial. If you are to overcome the dilemma, it will not be by your feelings, but by your faith.

First John 5:4 says, *"For whatever is born of God overcomes the world. And this is the victory that has overcome the world—our faith."* Yes, it is the shield of faith that quenches the fiery darts of the devil (see Eph. 6:16). The term "quench" means "to extinguish." Are there any fires brewing that you would like to extinguish? Your faith will do the job. If faith doesn't deliver you from it, then it will surely deliver you through it.

Now no chastening seems to be joyful for the present, but painful; nevertheless, afterward it yields the peaceable fruit of righteousness... (HEBREWS 12:11-12).

———•◦•———

THE FIRST LAUGH—The Laugh of Unbelief

Abraham and Sarah were already very old, and Sarah was past the age of childbearing. So Sarah laughed to herself as she thought, "After I am worn out and my lord is old, will I now have this pleasure?" Then the Lord said to Abraham, "Why did Sarah laugh and say, 'Will I really have a child, now that I am old?' Is anything too hard for the Lord? I will return to you at the appointed time next year, and Sarah will have a son" (Genesis 18:11-14 NIV).

THE LAST LAUGH—The Laugh of a Miracle

Sarah became pregnant and bore a son to Abraham in his old age, at the very time God had promised him. Abraham gave the name Isaac to the son Sarah bore him. When his son Isaac was eight days old, Abraham circumcised him, as God commanded him. Abraham was a hundred years old when his son Isaac was born to him. Sarah said, "God has brought me laughter, and everyone who hears about this will laugh with me" (Genesis 21:2-6 NIV).

"Come now, and let us reason together," says the Lord, "Though your sins are like scarlet, they shall be as white as snow; though they are red like crimson, they shall be as wool" (ISAIAH 1:18).

The slate has been cleansed at Calvary, but the mind is being renewed from day to day. As images came from time to time with flashbacks of things that haunted my mind like ghosts unexorcised, I began to seek the Lord who saved me for the grace to keep me. It was then that I began to realize the great truth that the blood of Christ doesn't just reach backward into the bleakness of my past debauchery—it also has the power to cover my ongoing struggles!

The blood of Christ covers my past, present, and future struggles—not so I could run through my inheritance like the prodigal son, but so I might have a comfort as I lie on the table of His grace. I must relax in this comfort and assurance and allow the tools of day-to-day tests and struggles to skillfully implant into my heart and mind a clearer reflection of His divine nature in me.

The fear of the Lord leads to life; then one rests content, untouched by trouble (PROVERBS 19:23 NIV).

———•○•———

Between the announcement that Sarah would bear a child and when she gave birth, everything in her was tested. Sarah followed Abraham out of their country and away from their kindred. Later, she takes another pilgrimage into what could have been a great tragedy. Abraham leads his wife into Gerar. As I am a man and a leader myself, I dare not be too hard on him. Anyone can make a poor decision. The decision to go to Gerar I could defend, even though Gerar means "halting place." I have made decisions that brought me to a halting place in my life. What's reprehensible is that Abraham, Sarah's protector and covering, when afraid for his own safety, lied about her identity (see Gen. 20). You never know who people are until you witness them under pressure. Abraham had a flagrant disregard for truth. And it was a life-threatening lie.

Sarah's love for Abraham gave her the courage to leave home, but her love for God brought forth the promised seed.

From that time on Jesus began to explain to his disciples that he must go to Jerusalem and suffer many things at the hands of the elders, the chief priests and the teachers of the law, and that he must be killed and on the third day be raised to life (MATTHEW 16:21 NIV).

━━━•◦•━━━

Faith is a key issue for Christians. The people of the early Church were simply called believers in recognition of their great faith. We need to understand the distinctions of faith. Faith cannot alter purpose; it only acts as an agent to assist in fulfilling the predetermined purpose of God. Faith becomes the vehicle that enables us to persevere and delivers us through the test. Faith guards the purpose of God. It will deliver us out of the hand of the enemy—the enemy being anything that hinders the purpose of God in our lives.

Hebrews chapter 11 discusses the definition of faith. It then shares the deeds of faith in verses 32-35a, and finally it discusses the perseverance of faith in verses 35b-39. There are distinctions of faith as well. Hebrews 11:32-35a emphasizes the distinct faith that escapes peril and overcomes obstacles.

No temptation has overtaken you except what is common to mankind. And God is faithful; he will not let you be tempted beyond what you can bear. But when you are tempted, he will also provide a way out so that you can endure it (I CORINTHIANS 10:13 NIV).

———•○•———

Have you ever known someone upon whom you had cast the weight of your confidence, only to have your trust defrauded in a moment of self-gratification and indulgence? Someone who has a selfish need can jeopardize all that you have.

Abraham's lie jeopardized the safety of his wife. King Abimelech was a heathen king. He was used to getting whatever he wanted. His reputation for debauchery preceded him so that Abraham, the father of faith, feared for his life. Rather than risk himself, he told the king that his wife was really his sister. Abraham knew that this would cause Sarah to have to fulfill the torrid desires of a heathenist. Her Abraham failed her. But God did not!

Maybe there is someone in your life who selfishly threw you into a tempestuous situation. Take courage! Just because satan has set a snare doesn't mean you can't escape. The God we serve is able.

And raised us up together, and made us sit together in the heavenly places in Christ Jesus, that in the ages to come He might show the exceeding riches of His grace in His kindness toward us in Christ Jesus (EPHESIANS 2:6-7).

—————◆•◇•◆—————

I appreciate the peace that comes from knowing I am His child. I am His—even when I feel like a mess, even when I am embarrassed, for His grace is sufficient for me. I thank Him for the peace He gives to every believer who matures into a trust-filled relationship with Jesus Christ. My initial surgery may be completed, but daily I remain under His intensive care as He monitors my progressions and occasional digressions. I wouldn't trust my future with anybody but Him.

You will never worship God correctly if you live in the shadows, wrestling with unconfessed sin. Whatever you do, there is an ever-increasing need for you to find a place of comfort in the presence of the Lord. It is possible to escape my presence, but not His. He is ever present, waiting on you to stand before Him and be healed.

Let your gentleness be evident to all. The Lord is near. Do not be anxious about anything, but in every situation, by prayer and petition, with thanksgiving, present your requests to God (PHILIPPIANS 4:5-6 NIV).

---◦◦◦---

Abraham's faith had always been the star of the Old Testament, but not that day. It's amazing how faith will come up in your heart at a crisis. Abraham passed off Sarah as his sister to King Abimelech, knowing she would become part of the royal harem.

Consider Sarah. She is facing the anxious footsteps of her rapist. She knows it will not be long until she will be abused. Like a frightened rabbit, she realizes Abraham will not rescue her. I don't know what she prayed, but I know she cried out to the only One she had left! Maybe she said, "God of Abraham, I need you to be my God too. Save me from this pending fate." Or maybe she cried, "O God! Have mercy on me!" Whatever she said, God heard her.

He will hear you as well. You don't have time to be angry or bitter. You've just got enough time to pray. Call out to Him. He is your God too!

What is more, I consider everything a loss because of the surpassing worth of knowing Christ Jesus my Lord, for whose sake I have lost all things. I consider them garbage, that I may gain Christ and be found in him... (PHILIPPIANS 3:8-9 NIV).

———•◦•———

There are times in our lives when God will take us from one realm of faith to another. Christ knows what kind of heat to place upon us to produce the faith needed in the situation. When we present our bodies as living sacrifices, He is the God who answers by fire. The good news lies in the fact that when our faith collapses beneath the weight of unbelievable circumstances, He gives us His faith to continue.

As the fire of persecution forces us to make deeper levels of commitment, our faith needs to be renewed to match our level of commitment. There is a place in God where the fire consumes every other desire but to know the Lord in the power of His resurrection. All other pursuits tarnish and seem worthless in comparison. Perhaps this is what Paul really pressed toward, that place of total surrender.

It is of the Lord's mercies that we are not consumed, because His compassions fail not. They are new every morning: great is Thy faithfulness. (LAMENTATIONS 3:22-23 KJV).

———•◦•———

Forgive me for condemning and judging anybody else. I know that if it were not for Your mercy, I would be guilty of the very things for which I have disdained others. Help me not to be hypocritical.

This kind of prayer and confession enhances your relationship with God as you begin to realize that you were saved by grace; you are saved by grace; and you will be saved by grace! Knowing this, how can you not be grateful? You know that He loves you so much that He stays in the house you haven't fully cleaned. He hates the acts; He despises the thoughts; but He loves the thinker.

God knows all our business and all our thoughts parade around naked before His scrutinizing eyes. We need a high priest for all the garbage and information that the Holy Spirit is privy to, yet others would never know. What greater compassion can be displayed than how God, through Christ, can be touched by how I feel.

> *But Jesus turned him about, and when he saw her, he said, Daughter, be of good comfort; thy faith hath made thee whole. And the woman was made whole from that hour.* (MATTHEW 9:22 KJV).

<hr />

O ne of the greatest deliverances people can ever experience in life is to have their attitude delivered. It doesn't do you any good to be delivered financially if your attitude doesn't change. I can give you $5,000, but if your attitude, your mental perspective, doesn't change, you will be broke in a week because you'll lose it again. The problem is not how much you have, it's what you do with what you have. If you can change your attitude, you might have only $50, but you'll take that $50 and learn how to get $5 million.

When God comes to heal, He wants to heal your emotions also. Sometimes all we pray about is our situation. We bring God our shopping list of desires. Fixing circumstances is like applying a Band-Aid, though. Healing attitudes set people free to receive wholeness.

You might think that the greatest deliverance is physical deliverance. Another deliverance that was even greater—that of an attitude change.

Not that we are sufficient of ourselves to think of anything as being from ourselves, but our sufficiency is from God, who also made us sufficient as ministers of the new covenant (2 CORINTHIANS 3:5-6).

---•◦•---

Time has hidden the future of a baby deeply within the tiny hands that someday will be different things to different people. "Who is this child?" the parents ponder. "When we are old, who will this child be? What is the level of contribution we have given to this world?" Time listens quietly, but still offers no answer.

The haunting question dulls with time, but still hums beneath the mind of the mature. "Who am I?" We have a deep need to find an answer. We are very interested in ourselves. Many of us come to know the Lord because we desperately need to know ourselves. Does that seem strange? It isn't, really. If we have a problem with an appliance, we always refer to the owner's manual. In our case it's the Bible. When repairs are needed, we go to the Manufacturer. Psalm 100 says, *"It is He who has made us, and not we ourselves"* (Ps. 100:3).

But I am poor and needy; yet the Lord thinks upon me. You are my help and my deliverer; do not delay, O my God (PSALM 40:17).

———•○•———

Can you imagine how hard life was for the infirm woman who was bent over? (See Luke 13.) She had to struggle, because of her problem, to come to Jesus. Few of us are crippled in the same way. However, we all face crippling limitations. We can be bowed over financially. We can be bowed over emotionally. We can be bowed over where we have no self-esteem. He wants to see us struggling toward Him. Jesus could have walked to this woman, but He chose not to. He wants to see us struggle toward Him.

He wants you to want Him enough to overcome obstacles and to push in His direction. He doesn't want to just throw things at you that you don't have a real conviction to receive. When you see a humped-over person crawling through the crowd, know that that person really wants help. That kind of desire is what it takes to change your life. Jesus is the answer. It doesn't matter what the problem is, He is the answer.

Whenever I am afraid, I will trust in You (PSALM 56:3).

———•○•———

Fear is as lethal to us as paralysis of the brain. It makes our thoughts become arthritic and our memory sluggish. It is the kind of feeling that can make a graceful person stumble up the stairs in a crowd. You know what I mean—the thing that makes the articulate stutter and the rhythmic become spastic. Like an oversized growth, fear soon becomes impossible to camouflage. Telltale signs like trembling knees or quivering lips betray fear even in the most disciplined person.

Fear traps time and holds it hostage in a prison of icy anxiety. Eventually, though, like the thawing of icicles on a roof, a heart can gradually melt into a steady and less pronounced beat.

I confess that maturity has chased away many of the ghosts and goblins of my youthful closet of fear. Nevertheless, there are still those occasional moments when reason gives way to the fanciful imagination of the fearful little boy in me, who peeks his head out of my now fully developed frame like a turtle sticks his head out of its shell with caution and precision.

And begged Him that they might only touch the hem of His garment. And as many as touched it were made perfectly well (MATTHEW 14:36).

————•◦•————

There's a place in God where the Lord will touch you and provide intimacy in your life when you're not getting it from other places. You must be open to His touch. If you can't receive from Him, you may find yourself like the woman at the well, who sought physical gratification (see John 4:18). If you seek only the physical when you really need intimacy, what you end up getting is simply sex. Sex is a poor substitute for intimacy. It's nice with intimacy, but when it is substituted for intimacy, it's frustrating.

Likewise, we are snared by the words in our own mouth. The enemy would love to destroy you with your own words. He will use your strength against you. Many of you have beat yourself down with the power of your own words. The enemy worked you against yourself until you saw yourself as crippled. Reverse his plan. If you had enough force to bend yourself, you've got enough force to straighten yourself back up again.

The Gentiles shall see your righteousness, and all kings your glory. You shall be called by a new name, which the mouth of the Lord will name (ISAIAH 62:2).

———————•○•———————

Jacob was his mother's darling. He was what we would call a "momma's boy." Jacob, whose name meant "supplanter" or "trickster," literally "con man," was left alone with God. God cannot accomplish anything with us until we are left alone with Him. There, in the isolation of our internal strife, God begins the process of transforming disgrace into grace. It only took a midnight rendezvous and an encounter with a God he couldn't "out slick" to bring Jacob's leg to a limp and his fist to a hand clasped in prayer. "I won't let You go till You bless me," he cries. God then tells him what he really needs to know. He tells Jacob that he is not who he thinks he is. In fact, he is really Israel, a prince. (See Genesis 32:24-30.)

My friend, when we, like Jacob, seek to know God, He will inevitably show us our real identity. My friend, if no one else knows who you are, God knows.

The Lord is my light and my salvation; whom shall I fear? The Lord is the strength of my life; of whom shall I be afraid? When the wicked, even mine enemies and my foes, came upon me to eat up my flesh, they stumbled and fell (PSALM 27:1-2).

———•○•———

Sometimes pain can become too familiar. Ungodly relationships often become familiar. Change doesn't come easily. Habits and patterns are hard to break. Sometimes we maintain relationships because we fear change. However, when we see our value the way Jesus sees us, we muster the courage to break away.

He will defend you before your critics. Now is the time for you to focus on receiving the miraculous and getting the water that you could not get before. He is loosing you to water. You haven't been drinking for 18 years, but now you can get a drink. With Jesus, you can do it.

Some of you have been a packhorse for many years. People have dumped on you. You've never been allowed to develop without stress and weights, not just because of the circumstances, but because of how deeply things affect you. Our God, however, is a liberator.

My dear children, for whom I am again in the pains of childbirth until Christ is formed in you (GALATIANS 4:19 NIV).

---•◦•---

God understands the hidden part within us. In spite of our growth, income, education, or notoriety, He still speaks to the childhood issues of the aging heart. This is the ministry that only a Father can give.

The Lord looks beyond our facade and sees the trembling places in our lives. He knows our innermost needs. No matter how spiritually mature we try to appear, He is still aware that lurking in the shadows is a discarded desire we just prayed off last night—the lingering evidence of some temper or temptation that only the Father can see hiding within His supposedly "all grown-up" little child.

It is He alone who can see the very worst in us, yet still think the very best of us. It is the unfailing love of a Father whose son should have been old enough to receive his inheritance without acting like a child, without wandering off into failure. Nevertheless, the Father's love throws a party for the prodigal and prepares a feast for the foolish. Comprehend with childhood faith the love of the Father!

The Lord had said to Abram, "Go from your country, your people and your father's household to the land I will show you. "I will make you into a great nation, and I will bless you; I will make your name great, and you will be a blessing (GENESIS 12:1-2 NIV).

———◦———

Yಠou must reach the point where it is the Lord whom you desire. Singleness of heart will bring about deliverance. Perhaps you have spent all your time and effort trying to prove yourself to someone who is gone. Maybe an old lover left you with scars. The person may be dead and buried, but you are still trying to win approval.

In this case, you are dedicated to worthless tasks. You are committed to things, unattainable goals, that will not satisfy. Christ must be your ambition. For some things you don't have time to recover gradually. The moment you get the truth, you are loosed.

Once you realize that you have been unleashed, you will feel a sudden change. When you come to Jesus, He will motivate you. You need to blossom and come forth.

Set your mind on things above, not on things on the earth. For you died, and your life is hidden with Christ in God (COLOSSIANS 3:2-3).

———•○•———

The new birth is not a change on your birth certificate; it is a change in your heart. In this sense we have a name change as it pertains to our character.

A name is important. It tells something about your origin or your destiny. You don't want just anyone to name you. Many of God's people are walking under the stigma of their old nature's name. That wretched feeling associated with what others called you or thought about you can limit you as you reach for greatness. However, it is not what others think that matters. You want to be sure, even if you are left alone and no one knows but you, to know who the Father says you are. Knowing your new name is for your own edification. When the enemy gets out his list and starts naming your past, tell him, "Haven't you heard? The person you knew died! I am not who he was and I am certainly not what he did!"

We give thanks to God always for you all, making mention of you in our prayers; remembering without ceasing your work of faith, and labor of love, and patience of hope in our Lord Jesus Christ, in the sight of God and Father (I THESSALONIANS 1:2-3).

———◦———

Faith is an equal opportunity business. There is no discrimination in it. Faith will work for you. When you approach God, don't worry about the fact that you are a woman. Never become discouraged on that basis when it comes to seeking Him. You will only get as much from God as you can believe Him for.

He wants you to believe Him. He is trying to teach you so when the time for a real miracle does come, you'll have some faith to draw from. God wants you to understand that if you can believe Him, you can go from defeat to victory and from poverty to prosperity!

Faith is more than a fact—faith is an action. When you finally understand that you are loose, you will start behaving as if you were set free. You are whole; you are loose. You can go anywhere.

He shall feed His flock like a shepherd: He shall gather the lambs with His arm, and carry them in His bosom, and shall gently lead those that are with young (ISAIAH 40:11 KJV).

When the disciples asked Jesus to teach them to pray, the first thing He taught them was to acknowledge the fatherhood of God. When we say "Our Father," we acknowledge His fatherhood and declare our sonship. We need to know not only who our father is, but how he feels about us.

I can still remember what it was like to fall asleep watching television and have my father carry me up the stairs to bed. I never felt as safe and protected as I did in the arms of my father—that is, until he died and I was forced to seek refuge in the arms of my Heavenly Father.

What a relief to learn that God can carry the load even better than my natural father could, and that He will never leave me nor forsake me! Perhaps this inspired the hymnist to pen, "What a fellowship, what a joy divine. Leaning on the everlasting arms" ("Leaning On the Everlasting Arms," Elisha A. Hoffman, 1887).

Now faith is the substance of things hoped for, the evidence of things not seen. For by it the elders obtained a good testimony (HEBREWS 11:1-2).

———•○•———

Hebrews chapter 11 is a faith "hall of fame." It lists great people of God who believed Him and accomplished great exploits. There are two contrasting women mentioned in the faith "hall of fame." Sarah, Abraham's wife, is listed. Rahab, the Jericho prostitute, is listed as well. A married woman and a whore made it to the hall of fame. A godly woman and a whore made it into the book. I understand why Sarah was included, but how in the world did this prostitute get to be honored? She was listed because God does not honor morality. He honors faith. That was the one thing they had in common; nothing else.

Rahab didn't have a husband. She had the whole city. Sarah stayed in the tent and knit socks. There was no similarity in their lifestyles, just in their faith. God saw something in Sarah that He also saw in Rahab. Do not accept the excuse that because you have lived like a Rahab you can't have the faith experience.

Even if you had ten thousand guardians in Christ, you do not have many fathers, for in Christ Jesus I became your father through the gospel (I CORINTHIANS 4:15 NIV).

━━━━●•○•●━━━━

We must know the difference between guardians and fathers. Paul said that he became their father through the Gospel. What does this mean?

Boys are nurtured by their mothers, but they receive their identity and definition of masculinity from their fathers! Thank God for the mothers in the Church—but where are our fathers? We have raised a generation of young men who couldn't find their natural fathers and now they struggle with their spiritual fathers.

It is difficult to develop healthy spiritual authority in the heart of a man who hasn't seen healthy male relationships. Such men tend to be overly sensitive or rebellious, quickly associating authority with abuse as that may be their only past experience. To you men, whether younger or older, who still wrestle with these issues, allow the hand of your Heavenly Father to heal the abuse and neglect of your earthly fathers. God is so wise that He will give you a spiritual father to fill the voids in your life. Trust Him!

Looking unto Jesus the author and finisher of our faith... (HEBREWS 12:2).

———— •○• ————

God wants you to believe Him. Make a decision and stand on it. Rahab decided to take a stand on the side of God's people. She hid the spies. She made the decision based on her faith. She took action. Faith is a fact and faith is an action. She took action because she believed God would deliver her when Jericho fell to the Israelites.

God wants your faith to be developed. Faith is an equal opportunity business. No matter how many mistakes you have made, it is still faith that God honors. You may have been like Rahab, but if you can believe God, He will save your house. You know, He didn't save only her; He saved her entire household. All the other homes in Jericho were destroyed.

You would have thought He would have saved some nice little lady's house. Perhaps He would have saved some cottage housing an old woman, or a little widow's house, with petunias growing by the sidewalk. No, God saved the whore's house. Was it because He wanted it? No, He wanted the faith. That is what moves God.

To know the love of Christ which passes knowledge; that you may be filled with all the fullness of God (EPHESIANS 3:19).

The Bible declares that we should have a strong degree of reverence for God. "Reverence" means to respect or revere; "fear" has the connotation of terror and intimidation. That kind of fear is not a healthy attitude for a child of God to have about his Heavenly Father. The term rendered "fear" in Job 28:28 could be better translated as "respect."

Fear will drive people away from God like it drove Adam to hide in the bushes at the sound of the voice of his only Deliverer. Adam said, *"I heard Thy voice in the garden, and I was afraid..."* (Gen. 3:10 KJV). That is not the reaction a loving father wants from his children. I don't want my children to scatter and hide when I approach! I may not always agree with what they have done, but I will always love who they are. He may not approve of your conduct, but He still loves you! In fact, when you come to understand this fact, it will help you improve your conduct.

But my righteous one will live by faith. And I take no pleasure in the one who shrinks back (HEBREWS 10:38 NIV).

———•◦•———

I f you believe that your background will keep you from moving forward with God, then you don't understand the value of faith. The thing God is asking from you is faith. Some may live good, clean, separated lives.

If you want to grasp the things of God, you will not be able to purely because of your lifestyle, but because of your conviction. God gave healing to some folks who weren't even saved. They were sinners. Perhaps some of them never did get saved, but they got healed because they believed Him.

And Joshua saved Rahab the harlot alive, and her father's household, and all that she had; and she dwelleth in Israel even unto this day; because she hid the messengers, which Joshua sent to spy out Jericho (Joshua 6:25 KJV).

There was something in Rahab's house that God called valuable. Faith was there. The thing that moves God is faith. If you believe Him, He will move in your life according to your faith and not to your experience.

Now it came to pass, when she was in hard labor, that the midwife said to her, "Do not fear; you will have this son also." And so it was, as her soul was departing (for she died), *that she called his name Ben-Oni; but his father called him Benjamin* (GENESIS 35:17-18).

———•◦•———

Jacob, now Israel, has come to a point of resting in his God-given identity. Israel has seasoned and matured. He has produced many strong sons. One son is yet inside the love of his life, Rachel, who is in the final stages of pregnancy. Before they could reach their destination, Rachel births a son. Just before she dies, Rachel looks at her baby and names him Ben-Oni, which means "son of my sorrow."

Jacob's eyes turn deeply within. Perhaps he remembers what a wrong name can do to a child. He speaks with the wisdom that is born out of personal experience. "He shall not be called Ben-Oni, son of my sorrow. He shall be called Benjamin, son of my right hand. He is my strength, not my sorrow!" he declares. Guess whose name prevailed, Benjamin; you are who your father says you are.

Ask, and it shall be given you; seek, and ye shall find; knock, and it shall be opened unto you. For every one that asketh receiveth; and he that seeketh findeth; and to him that knocketh it shall be opened (MATTHEW 7:7-8 KJV).

---◦---

Searching releases answers. Many things available to us will not be found without an all-out search. Seeking God also takes focus. This search has to be what the police call an A.P.B—an "all points bulletin." The entire department is asked to seek the same thing. Thus our search can't be a distracted, half-hearted curiosity. There must be something to produce a unified effort: body, soul, and spirit—all points—seeking the same thing. There is a blessing waiting for us. It will require an A.P.B. to bring it into existence, but it will be worth attaining. Who knows what God will release if we go on an all-out God-hunt.

The crucial times that arise in our lives require more than good advice. We need a word from God. There are moments when we need total seclusion. We come home from work, turn off the telephone, and lie before God for a closer connection.

Therefore God also has highly exalted Him and given Him the name which is above every name, that at the name of Jesus every knee should bow, of those in heaven, and of those on earth, and of those under the earth (PHILIPPIANS 2:9-10).

———— ◆○◆ ————

In the name of Jesus you must break the spell of every name that would attach itself to you. If your Heavenly Father didn't give you that name, then it isn't right. You are who He says you are. Rest in the identity that He places upon you. No one knew any better than Jacob/Israel the power of a name change! Remember, it was in his Father's presence that he discovered he was not a trickster, but a prince! When you believe on the covenant name of Jesus, you break the strength of every other name that would attach itself to your identity. In the early Church, entire cities were delivered from satanic attack in that name. Even today, drug addicts, lesbians, pimps, and every other name is subject to the name of the Lord. His name is strong enough to break the bondage of any other name that would attach itself to your life.

"Teacher," they said, "we know that You are a man of integrity and that You teach the way of God in accordance with the truth. You aren't swayed by others, because You pay no attention to who they are" (MATTHEW 22:16 NIV).

———•◦•———

The mind is continually being reconstructed by the Holy Spirit to enable you to soar above your past.

Christ has a balanced mind. He doesn't suffer from low self-esteem. He "thought it not robbery" to be equal with God (see Phil. 2:5-7). For Him, being equal with God was and is a reality. That might seem a little extreme for you and me. He was comfortable with His exaltation. He didn't allow opinions of other men to determine who He "thought" He was. His inner perception was fixed.

The miracle of His strength is that, unlike most people who are that strong about their inner worth, Christ Jesus did not wrestle with arrogance. He knew who He was, yet He *"made Himself of no reputation"* (Phil. 2:7). When you have healthy thoughts about your own identity, it frees you from the need to impress other people. Their opinion ceases to be the shrine where you worship!

And God shall wipe away all tears from their eyes; and there shall be no more death, neither sorrow, nor crying, neither shall there be any more pain: for the former things are passed away. And He that sat upon the throne said, Behold, I make all things new (REVELATION 21:4-5 KJV).

———•○•———

If you are wrestling with the curse and stigma of public opinion, you don't have to stay the way you are. The Potter wants to put you back together again. God is a God of second chances.

This good news is that God changes names. Throughout the Scriptures He took men like Abram, the exalted father, and transformed his image and character into Abraham, the father of many nations. There is a place in your walk with God—a place of discipleship—whereby God radically changes your character. With that change He can erase the stigma of your past and give you a fresh name in your community—but most importantly, in your heart. Get on your knees and wrestle with Him in prayer until you can arise knowing what He knows. Rise up from prayer knowing who you really are in the Spirit and in the Kingdom.

The eyes of your understanding being enlightened;
that you may know what is the hope of His calling,
what are the riches of the glory of His inheritance in
the saints (EPHESIANS 1:18).

Y ou want the inheritance of your father to pass on to you. Why should you sit there and be in need when your Father has left you everything? Your Father is rich, and He left everything to you. However, you will not get your inheritance until you ask for it. Demand what your father left you. That degree, that promotion, that financial breakthrough has your name on it.

The power to get wealth is in your tongue. You shall have whatever you say. If you keep sitting around murmuring, groaning, and complaining, you use your tongue against yourself. Open your mouth and speak something good about yourself. Begin to speak deliverance and power. You are not defeated. You are Abraham's heir.

When you start speaking correctly, God will give you what you say. You say you want it. God willed you something. Your Father left you an inheritance. God blesses all children of Abraham as His own.

I have come in My Father's name, and you do not receive Me; if another comes in his own name, him you will receive (JOHN 5:43).

———•◦•———

The Word of the Lord often stands alone. It has no attorney and it needs no witness. It can stand on its own merit. Whatever He says, you are! If you are to fight the challenge of this age, then shake the enemy's names and insults off your shoulder. Look the enemy in the eye without guilt or timidity and declare:

"I have not come clothed in the vesture of my past. Nor will I use the opinions of this world for my defense. No, I am far wiser through the things I have suffered. Therefore I have come in my Father's name. He has anointed my head, counseled my fears, and taught me who I am. I am covered by His anointing, comforted by His presence, and kept by His auspicious grace. Today, as never before, I stand in the identity He has given me and renounce every memory of who I was yesterday. I was called for such a time as this, and I have come in my Father's name!"

If you do not stand firm in your faith, you will not stand at all (ISAIAH 7:9 NIV).

———•◦•———

The Lord is your defense. You do not have to defend yourself. When God has delivered you, do not stop what you're doing to answer your accusers. Continue to bless His name, because you do not want your attitude to become defensive. When you have been through difficult times, you cannot afford to play around with moods and attitudes. Depression and defensiveness may make you vulnerable to the devil.

When you get to the point that you quit defending yourself or attacking others, you open up a door for the Lord to fight for you.

When you're in trouble, God will reach into the mess and pull you out. However, you must be strong enough not to let people drag you back into it. Once God unleashes you, don't let anyone trap you into some religious fight. Keep praising Him. The more people criticize you, the more you should just stand and keep believing God. God is trying to get you to a place of faith. He is trying to deliver you from an attitude of negatives.

Know ye not that ye are the temple of God, and that the Spirit of God dwelleth in you? If any man defile the temple of God, him shall God destroy; for the temple of God is holy, which temple ye are (I CORINTHIANS 3:16-17 KJV).

---◦---

Most of us come to the Lord damaged. We're dead spiritually, damaged emotionally, and decaying physically. When He saved you, He quickened, or made alive, your dead spirit. He also promised you a new body. Then He began the massive renovation necessary to repair your damaged thoughts about life, about others, and about yourself—here come all types of nails, saws, levels, bricks, and blocks.

We all need the Lord to help us with ourselves. We came to Him as condemned buildings, and He reopened the places that satan thought would never be inhabited. The Holy Spirit moved in, but He brought His hammers and His saw with Him.

While we dress and smell nice outwardly, people do not hear the constant hammering and sawing going on inwardly, as the Lord works within us, trying desperately to meet a deadline and present us as a newly constructed masterpiece fit for the Master's use.

Therefore, having been justified by faith, we have peace with God through our Lord Jesus Christ, through whom also we have access by faith into this grace in which we stand, and rejoice in hope of the glory of God (ROMANS 5:1-2).

———•○•———

Some of us have particular problems based on where we came from. We've got to deal with it. God says there is neither Greek nor Jew. There is no such thing as a Black church. There is no such thing as a White church. It's only one Church, purchased by the blood of the Lamb. We are all one in Christ Jesus.

You may have been born with a silver spoon in your mouth too, but it doesn't make any difference. In the Kingdom of God, social status doesn't mean anything. Faith is the only thing in this world where there is true equal opportunity. Everyone can come to Jesus.

"There is neither male nor female" (Gal. 3:28). God doesn't look at your gender. He looks at your heart. He doesn't look at morality and good works. He looks at the faith that lives within. God is looking in your heart. All people are one in Christ Jesus.

Behold, children are a heritage from the Lord, the fruit of the womb is a reward. Like arrows in the hand of a warrior, so are the children of one's youth. Happy is the man who has his quiver full of them... (PSALM 127:3-5).

———•○•———

The psalmist David wrote a brief note that speaks to the heart of men about their attitude toward their offspring. David is the man who prayed feverishly for mercy as his child squirmed in the icy hands of death. If anybody knows the value of children, it is those who just left theirs in the ground. *"Like arrows in the hand of a warrior, so are the children of one's youth,"* says King David whose arrow they lowered in the ground.

Why did he compare children to arrows? Maybe it was for their potential to be propelled into the future. Maybe he was trying to tell us that children go where we, their parents, aim them. Parents must be responsible to place them in the kind of bow that will accelerate their success and emotional well-being. How happy I am to have a quiver full of arrows.

Seek the Lord while He may be found, call upon Him while He is near. Let the wicked forsake his way, and the unrighteous man his thoughts; and let him return to the Lord, and He will have mercy on him; and to our God, for He will abundantly pardon (ISAIAH 55:6-7).

———•◦•———

Unfortunately, it generally takes devastation on a business level to make most men commit more of their interest in relationships. Job probably could have reached out to his children for comfort, but he had lost them too. His marriage had deteriorated to the degree that Job said his wife abhorred his breath (see Job 19:17). Then he also became ill. Have you ever gone through a time in your life when you felt you had been jinxed? Everything that could go wrong, did! Frustration turns into alienation. So now what? Will you use this moment to seek God or to brood over your misfortune? With the right answer, you could turn the jail into a church!

If the storms keep coming, the lightning flashes, and the thunder thumps, what matters is keeping the waters out of the inside. Keep that stuff out of your spirit!

*Let them melt away as waters which run continually:
when he bendeth his bow to shoot his arrows...*
(PSALM 58:7 KJV).

———•◦•———

It is for the arrows of this generation that we must
pray—they who are being aimed at the streets and
drugs and perversion. Not all of them, but some of
them have been broken in the quiver!

If someone must be hurt, if it ever becomes necessary to bear pains or withstand trials, let it be adults
and not children. I can accept the fate before me. I
was my father's arrow and my mother's heart. My
father is dead, but his arrows are yet soaring in the
wind. You will never know him; he is gone. However,
my brother, my sister, and I are scientific proof that he
was, and through us, continues to be. I am an arrow
shot. I have had the greatest riches known to man. I
have had an opportunity to test the limits of my destiny. Whether preferred or rejected, let the record
show: I am here. Oh, God, let me hit my target! But if
I miss and plummet to the ground, then at least I can
say, "I have been shot!"

For His anger is but for a moment, His favor is for life; weeping may endure for a night, but joy comes in the morning (PSALM 30:5).

━━━●○●━━━

David said that if we could hold out, joy comes in the morning. The bad news is, everybody has a bad night at one time or another. The good news is there will be a morning after. Allow the joy of the morning light to push away any unwanted partners, curses, or fears that stop you from achieving your goal.

So let the hungry mouth of failure's offspring meet the dry breast of a Christian who has determined to overcome the past. In order for these embryos of destruction to survive, they must be fed. They feed on the fears and insecurities of people who haven't declared their liberty.

Once you realize that you are the source from which it draws its milk, you regain control. Feed what you want to live and starve what you want to die! Why not think positively until every negative thing that is a result of dead issues turns blue and releases its grip on your home and your destiny? It's your mind. You've got the power.

The Spirit of God has made me, and the breath of the Almighty gives me life (JOB 33:4).

———•◦•———

In the ministry, there is a different prerequisite for effectiveness than what the textbooks alone can provide. It is not a medicine compiled by a pharmacist that is needed for the patients lying on the tables of my heart. We don't need medicine; we need miracles. Many have more faith in a textbook written by a person whose eyes may be clouded by their own secrets, than to rely upon the Word of a God who knows the end from the beginning.

If there is something minor wrong with my car, like a radiator hose needing replaced or a tire changed, I can take it almost anywhere. But if I suspect there is trouble with it, I always take it to the dealer. The manufacturer knows his product better than the average mechanic. So like the dealership, ministers may work with, but need not be intimidated by, the sciences of the mind! God is not practicing. He is accomplished. I want to share Godgiven, biblical answers to troubling questions as we deal with the highly sensitive areas of counseling.

For as he things in his heart, so is he (PROVERBS 23:7).

...if there is any virtue and if there is anything praiseworthy—meditate on these things (PHILIPPIANS 4:8).

———•◦•———

I n this verse, Paul teaches thought modification. He taught that if we exercise the discipline of thought modification, we can produce internal or intrinsic excellence. The phrase, "if there be any virtue," suggests that if there is to be any intrinsic excellence, we must modify our thoughts to think on the things he mentioned first.

The term "virtue" refers to intrinsic excellence. That means people who are filled with excellence achieve that excellence by the thoughts they have about themselves and about the world around them. Thoughts are powerful. They feed the seeds of greatness that are in the womb of our minds. They also can nurse the negative insecurities that limit us and exempt us from greatness. There is a virtue that comes from tranquil, peaceful thoughts that build positive character in the heart. As a rule, people who are cynical and vicious tend to be unsuccessful. If they are successful, they don't really feel their success because their cynicism robs from them the sweet taste of reward.

He hath made His wonderful works to be remembered: the Lord is gracious and full of compassion (PSALM 111:4 KJV).

I earnestly believe that where there is no compassion, there can be no lasting change. As long as Christian leadership secretly jeers and sneers at the perversion that comes into the Church, there will be no healing. The enemy robs us of our healing power by robbing us of our concern.

Compassion is the mother of miracles! When the storm had troubled the waters and Peter thought he would die, he didn't challenge Christ's power; he challenged His compassion. He went into the back side of the ship and said, *"Teacher, do You not care that we are perishing?"* (Mark 4:38). He understood that if there is no real compassion, then there can be no miracle.

Until we, as priests, are touched with the feelings of our parishioners' illnesses rather than just turned off by their symptoms, they will not be healed. The power to heal is in the power to care. Rise and be healed in the name of Jesus.

How precious also are Your thoughts to me, O God!
How great is the sum of them! (PSALM 139:17)

———◦———

Thoughts are powerful. They feed the seeds of greatness that are in the womb of our minds. They also can nurse the negative insecurities that limit us and exempt us from greatness. There is a virtue that comes from peaceful thoughts that build positive character in the heart. As a rule, people who are cynical and vicious tend to be unsuccessful. If they are successful, they don't really feel their success because their cynicism robs from them the sweet taste of reward.

Thoughts are secrets hidden behind quick smiles and professional veneers. They are a private world that others cannot invade. None of us would be comfortable at having all our thoughts played aloud for the whole world to hear. Yet our thoughts can accurately forecast approaching success or failure. No one can hear God think, but we can feel the effects of His thoughts toward us. Like sprouts emerging from enriched soil, our words and eventually our actions push through the fertilized fields of our innermost thoughts. Like our Creator, we deeply affect others by our thoughts toward them.

For My thoughts are not your thoughts, neither are your ways My ways, saith the Lord. For as the heavens are higher than the earth, so are My ways higher than your ways, and My thoughts than your thoughts (ISAIAH 55:8-9).

———•◦•———

We need to renew our minds daily in God's presence, for I believe that as we hear the thoughts of God, His thinking becomes increasingly contagious. It is so important that we have a relationship with Him. His Word becomes a lifeline thrown to a man who would otherwise drown in the swirling whirlpool of his own thoughts.

Job said that he esteemed God's Word more than his necessary food (see Job 23:12). As for me, God is my counselor. He talks with me about my deepest, darkest issues; He comforts the raging tide of my fears and inhibitions. What would we be if He would wax silent and cease to guide us through this perilous maze of mental mania? It is His soft words that turn away the wrath of our nagging memories. If He speaks to me, His words become symphonies of enlightenment falling like soft rain on a tin roof. They give rest and peace.

For the vision is yet for an appointed time, but at the end it shall speak, and not lie: though it tarry, wait for it; because it will surely come, it will not tarry (HABAKKUK 2:3).

———•◦•———

Quite honestly, there are moments when life feels like it has all the purpose of gross insanity. These are the times that try men's hearts. These are the times when we seek answers!

Like a desperate sailor trying to plug a leaking ship, Job frantically cast back and forth in his mind, looking for some shred, some fragment of hope. Exasperated, he sullenly sat in the stupor of his condition and sadly confessed, *"Look, I go forward, but He is not there"* (Job 23:8). "I can't find Him where I thought He would be." Have you ever told yourself that the storm would be over soon? And the sun came and the sun left, and still the same rains beat vehemently against the ship. It almost feels as if God missed His appointment. You thought He would move by now! Remember, dear friend, God doesn't synchronize His clock by your little mortal watch. He has a set time to bless you; just hold on.

He heals the brokenhearted and binds up their wounds (PSALM 147:3).

------•◦•------

Splintered, broken arrows come in all colors and forms. Some are black, some white; some are rich, some poor. One thing about pain, though: It isn't prejudiced. To God be the glory. He is a magnificent Healer!

Each person who has been through these adversities has her own story. Some have been blessed by not having to experience any such circumstance. Let the strong bear the infirmities of the weak. God can greatly use you to restore wholeness to others who walk in varying degrees of brokenness. To those who have fallen prey to satan's snares, we teach righteousness while still loving the unrighteous. Most of us have had some degree of damage. The fact that we have persevered is a testimony.

Anything hurt, is unhappy. We cannot get a wounded lion to jump through hoops! Hurting children and hurting adults can carry the unpleasant aroma of bitterness.

Even if you were exposed to grown-up situations when you were a child, God can reverse what you've been through. He'll let the grown-up person experience the joy of being a child in the presence of God!

> For the weapons of our warfare are not carnal but
> mighty in God for pulling down strongholds, casting
> down arguments and every high thing that exalts
> itself against the knowledge of God, bringing every
> thought into captivity to the obedience of Christ
> (2 CORINTHIANS 10:4-5).

---•◦•---

God has given you power over the enemy! He has given you the power to abort the seeds of failure. Pull down those things that have taken a strong hold in your life. If you don't pull them down, they will refuse to relinquish their grip. It will take an act of your will and God's power to stop the spiritual unborn from manifesting in your life. God will not do it without you—but He will do it through you.

The greatest freedom you have is the freedom to change your mind. Repentance is when the mind decides to overthrow the government that controlled it in the past. As long as these other things reign in your life, they are sitting on the throne. If they are on the throne, then Christ is on the Cross. Put Christ on the throne and your past on the Cross.

Then little children were brought to Him that He might put His hands on them and pray, but the disciples rebuked them (MATTHEW 19:13).

———•◦•———

I t is interesting to me that just before this took place the Lord was ministering on the subject of divorce and adultery. When He brought up that subject, someone brought the children to Him so He could touch them.

Who were these nameless persons who had the insight and the wisdom to bring the children to the Master? They brought the children to Him that He might touch them. What a strange interruption to a discourse on adultery and divorce. Here are these little children dragging dirty blankets and blank gazes into the presence of a God who is dealing with grown-up problems. He takes time from His busy schedule not so much to counsel them, but just to touch them. That's all it takes. Don't forget to touch their little lives with a word of hope and a smile of encouragement. It may be the only one some will receive. You are the builders of our future. Be careful, for you may be building a house that we will have to live in!

This people I have I formed for Myself; they shall declare My praise (ISAIAH 43:21).

———•◦•———

Above all titles and professions, every Christian is called to be a worshiper. We are a royal priesthood that might have become extinct had the mercy of the Lord not arrested the horrors of the enemy. Calloused hands are raised in praise—hands that tell a story of struggle, whether spiritual or natural. Who could better thank the Lord than the oppressed who were delivered by the might of a loving God whose love is tempered with the necessary ability to provoke change.

The intensity of our praise is born out of the ever-freshness of our memories, not so much of our past, but of His mercies toward us.

Woe be to the priest who tries to have a fresh worship experience while constantly reliving the dead issues of the past. In that case the memories become an obstacle around your neck. What would it matter for all the voices in the earth to commend you for your contributions, if God disagreed? Lift up your head and be blessed in the presence of the Lord. Nothing is nearly as important as ministering to the Lord.

Surely He shall deliver you from the snare of the fowler and from the perilous pestilence (PSALM 91:3).

———•○•———

God's Word will accomplish what it is sent out to do. God says, "I won't stop in the middle of the job. I will not give up on you. I will keep hammering until you are balanced in your thinking and whole in your judgments." No one would ever believe that you were initially in such a deplorable state! He covers you with His precious blood even while His Word works on you.

Most of the time God delivers us (or is in the process of delivering us) while we maintain a veil of secrecy to protect our reputations and public perceptions. Secular scholars would be appalled if they knew how many of us were in serious trouble when we came to our wit's end and submitted to the redemptive work of the Lord. It was He who delivered us out from under the stress and the strain of our crises. His power forces open the fowler's snare that entrapped the mind. His Word gives us the grace to seize the opportunity to escape and go on with our lives!

And such were some of you. But you were washed, but you were sanctified, but you were justified in the name of the Lord Jesus and by the Spirit of our God (I CORINTHIANS 6:11).

---◆·○·◆---

I n the early Church, the disciples experienced awesome displays of power that we don't seem to experience to the same degree. Few of us are walking in enough light to cast the kind of shadow that causes others to be healed. What is wrong? We have become a nation of priests who spend too much time touching the dead and not enough washing our hearts with pure water!

Give your heart a bath. Submerge it deeply into the purity of God's Word and scrub away the remaining debris of deathly ills and concerns. These may be stopping you from participating in the greatest move of God that this generation will ever see! A clouded heart cannot move into the realm of faith. It takes clarity to flow in divine authority. Satan knows that pureness of heart is necessary to see God. These distresses and stresses are spiritual cholesterol! They will stop the heart from being able to see God.

Because you would forget your misery, and remember it as waters that have passed away (JOB 11:16).

———•◦•———

I t is inconceivable to the injured that the injury can be forgotten. To forget isn't to develop amnesia. It is to reach a place where the misery is pulled from the memory as a stinger pulled out of an insect bite. Once the stinger is gone, healing is inevitable. This passage says that the memory is as *"waters that have passed away."* Stand in a stream with waters around your ankles. The waters that pass by you at that moment, you will never see again. So it is with the misery that has challenged your life: Let it go, let it pass away. The brilliance of morning is in sharp contrast to the darkness of night; simply stated, it was night, but now it is day. David understood the aftereffects of traumatic deliverance when he said, *"Weeping may endure for a night, but joy comes in the morning"* (Ps. 30:5).

It is when we become secure in our relationship with God that we begin to allow the past to fall from us as a garment. We remember it, but choose not to wear it!

And after my skin is destroyed, this I know, that in my flesh I shall see God, whom I shall see for myself, and my eyes shall behold, and not another. How my heart yearns within me! (JOB 19:26-27)

———•◦•———

I f the worshiper has so many unresolved issues on his heart, how can he see God?

This Scripture clearly draws a line of prerequisites necessary to see God in His fullest sense. God's invisibility doesn't refer to an inability to be seen as much as it does to your inability to behold Him. To the blind all things are invisible. How can I see this God who cannot be detected in my vision's periphery? Jesus taught that a pure heart could see God. No wonder David cried out, *"Create in me a clean heart..."* (Ps. 51:10).

The term used in Matthew 5:8 for "pure" comes from the Greek word *katharos,* which means "to clean out," much like a laxative. Don't carry around what God wants discarded. Get rid of *"every weight, and the sin which so easily ensnares us"* (Heb. 12:1)! What God wants to unveil to you is worth the cleaning up to see.

But now, O Lord, You are our Father; we are the clay, and You our potter; and all we the work of Your hand (ISAIAH 64:8).

---◆◇◆---

Where is the God who sent an earthquake into the valley of dry bones and put them together? (See Ezekiel 37.) Or where is the God of the clay, who remolds the broken places and mends the jagged edge? (See Isaiah 64:8.) The God we seek is never far away. The issue is not so much His presence as it is my perception. Many times deliverance doesn't cost God one action. Deliverance comes when my mind accepts His timing and purpose in my life.

In my hours of crises, many times I found myself searching for the place of rest rather than for the answer. If I can find God, my needs become insignificant in the light of His presence. What is a problem if God is there? Do you realize the power of God's presence? I hear many people speak about the acts of God, but have you ever considered the mere presence of God? He doesn't have to do anything but be there, and it is over!

If it is burned up, the builder will suffer loss but yet will be saved—even though only as one escaping through the flames (I CORINTHIANS 3:15 NIV).

---•◦•---

I f you gaze deep into a fire you will notice that the sparks leave the burning log as hot as the fire itself. They swirl into the chimney into the dark chambers above. But these flickering lights are soon extinguished by being separated from their source. How many Christians explode into the brilliancy of worship and praise, but are soon dark and cold, losing their first fire? Stay in the fire, my friend, where the other embers can share their heat with you and keep you ablaze! It is the fire of God that will assist you in burning up the off-spring, the oddities, and the obstacles of yesteryear.

Perhaps that is what happened in the fiery furnace with the Hebrew boys. The fire was on assignment. It could burn only what was an obstacle hindering those who refused to worship idols from worshiping God. Some people He saves from the fire; praise God for them. But all too often God saves most of us by the fire!

Because God wanted to make the unchanging nature of His purpose very clear to the heirs of what was promised, He confirmed it with an oath. God did this so that, by two unchangeable things in which it is impossible for God to lie, we who have fled to take hold of the hope offered to us may be greatly encouraged (HEBREWS 6:17-18 NIV).

———•○•———

Reach out and embrace the fact that God has been watching over you all of your life. My friend, He covers you and He blesses you! Rejoice in Him in spite of the broken places. God's grace is sufficient for your needs and your scars. He will anoint you with oil. May it bathe, heal, and strengthen you as never before.

There will be a time in your life when God nurtures you through crisis situations. You may not even realize how many times God has intervened to relieve the tensions and stresses of day-to-day living. Every now and then He does us a favor—something we didn't earn or can't even explain. He knows when the load is overwhelming. Many times He moves (it seems to us) just in the nick of time.

Whom God set forth as a propitiation by His blood, through faith, to demonstrate His righteousness, because in His forbearance God had passed over the sins that were previously committed (ROMANS 3:25).

———•○•———

God wants to bring you to a place of rest, where there is no pacing the floor, no glaring at those with whom you are involved, through frightened eyes.

There is no torment like inner torment. How can you run from yourself? No matter what you achieve in life, if the old ghosts are not laid to rest, you will not have any real sense of peace and inner joy. God says, *"None shall make thee afraid."* A *"perfect love casts out fear"!* (See Job 11:19 KJV and 1 John 4:18.) It is a miserable feeling to spend your life in fear. Fear can manifest itself in jealousy, depression, and many other distresses. As you allow the past to pass over you as waters moving in the sea, you will begin to live and rest in a new assurance. Take authority over every flashback and every dream that keeps you linked to the past. The peace of God will do a new thing in your life.

They shall be Mine," says the Lord of hosts, "On the day that I make them My jewels. And I will spare them as a man spares his own son who serves him (MALACHI 3:17).

————•○•————

I was raised in the rich, robust Appalachian mountains of West Virginia which was the backyard for many Indians in days gone by. During my childhood, occasionally either my classmates or myself would find old Indian memorabilia in the rocks and creek beds. The most common thing to find would be discarded arrowheads. Perhaps an Indian brave had thrown away the arrow, assuming he had gotten out of it all the possible use he could. Though worthless to him, it was priceless to us as we retrieved it from its hiding place and saved it. I believe that God gathers discarded children who, like arrows, have been thrown away from the quiver of vain and ruthless people.

The reconstructive hand of the Potter can mend the broken places in any life. Amidst affairs and struggles, needs and incidents, may the peace and calmness of knowing God cause the birth of fresh dreams. But most of all, it lays to rest old fears.

A man who has friends must himself be friendly, but a true friend sticks closer than a brother (PROVERBS 18:24).

———•○•———

Friendship is the last remaining sign of our fleeting childhood dreams. Different from family love, which is not chosen but accepted, this love gradually grows until one day an acquaintance has graduated into a friend. Love is the graduation diploma, whether discussed or hinted.

The world has lost the ability to appreciate the value of a friend. Only occasionally in the course of a lifetime do we meet the kind of friend who is more than an acquaintance. This kind of kindred spirit feels as warm and fitting as an old house shoe, with its personalized contours impressed upon soft fabric for the benefit of weary feet.

The tragedy is that we all yearn for, but seldom acquire, true trust and covenant. The truth is that real relationship is hard work. Your actions express the importance of the other person.

Every relationship undergoes adjustments. We never know the magnitude of a relationship's strength until it is tested by some threatening force. There must be a strong adhesive that can withstand the pressure and not be weakened by outside forces.

But as many as received Him, to them He gave the right to become children of God, to those who believe in His name (JOHN 1:12).

———•◦•———

M y twin sons were playing on the floor with a truck. Later, I noticed that the boys were now running an airplane down an imaginary runway. I asked, "What happened to the truck you were playing with?" They explained, "Daddy, this is a transformer! It can be transformed from what it was before into whatever we want it to be!"

Suddenly I realized that God had made the first transformer! He created man in such a way that He could pull a woman out of him without ever having to reach back into the dust. Out of one creative act God transformed the man into a marriage. Then He transformed the marriage into a family, the family into a society, etc. God never had to reach into the ground again because the power to transform was intrinsically placed into man. God placed certain things in us that must come out. Every word of our personal prophetic destiny is inside us. He has ordained us to be!

Thou has proved mine heart; Thou hast visited me in the night; Thou hast tried me, and shalt find nothing; I am purposed that my mouth shall not transgress (PSALM 17:3 KJV).

---◦---

There is a strong tie between thought and action. Some time ago, when we discovered the power of our words, we began to teach Christians to speak positively. That is good. The only problem is, we were thinking one thing while the mouth was confessing something else. The results were not rewarding.

The Scriptures tell us that *"with the heart one believes unto righteousness, and with the mouth confession is made unto salvation"* (Rom. 10:10). There is a strong tie between what is believed and what is confessed. Your thoughts have to align with your confession—otherwise your house is divided against itself! Even God works out of the reservoir of His own thoughts. He does not consider what others think about you. Some of those people don't even believe in God. Nevertheless, He doesn't work out of their thoughts; He works out of His own! Quit trying to change the minds of other people—change your own. Your works will come out of the healing of your thoughts!

A friend loves at all times, and a brother is born for adversity (PROVERBS 17:17).

———•◦•———

Part of what we want from relationships is to know that you won't leave, regardless of what is encountered—even if you discover my worst imperfection! Isn't the real question, "Can I be transparent with you, and be assured that my nudity has not altered your commitment to be my friend?" I know that someone reading this has given up on friendship, with its many expenses and desertions. If you will not believe me, then believe the Word of God. It is possible to attain real ,abiding friendship.

Even natural blood ties don't always wear as well as heart ties. The Bible says there is a kind of friend that *"sticketh closer than a brother"* (Prov. 18:24 KJV).

The obvious friend is the one who stands by you, honoring and affirming you. A true friend should desire to see me prosper in my marriage, in my finances, and in my health and spirituality. If these virtues are present in the relationship, then we can easily climb over the hurdles of personal imperfection. We transmit through warm exchanges of mutual affection, our celebration of friendship.

Before I formed you in the womb I knew you; before you were born I sanctified you; I ordained you a prophet to the nations (JEREMIAH 1:5).

———•○•———

Salvation as it relates to destiny is the God-given power to become what God has eternally decreed you were before the foundation of the world. Grace is God's divine enablement to accomplish predestined purpose. When the Lord tells Paul, *"My grace is sufficient for you..."* (2 Cor. 12:9), His power is not intimidated by your circumstances. You are empowered by God to accomplish goals that transcend human limitations! It is important that each person God uses realizes that they are able to accomplish what others cannot only because God gives them the grace to do so. Problems are not really problems to a person who has the grace to serve in a particular area.

The excellency of our gifts are of God and not of us. He doesn't need nearly as much of our contributions as we think He does. So it is God who works out the internal destinies of men. He gives us the power to become who we are eternally and internally.

No weapon that is formed against thee shall prosper; and every tongue that shall rise against thee in judgment thou shalt condemn (ISAIAH 54:17).

---•◦•---

If we could talk to the three Hebrews who survived the fiery furnace, perhaps they would describe their experience with the Lord in the midst of the fire in this manner:

"The fire was all over us. Our ropes were ablaze, but our skin seemed undisturbed. Then something moved over in the smoke and ashes. We were not alone! His presence brought comfort in the fire. It was His presence that created protection in the midst of the crisis. Now, we don't mean that the fire went out because He was there. No, it still burned. It was just that the burning wasn't worthy to be compared to the brilliancy of His presence. We never saw Him again. He only showed up when we needed Him most. But one thing was sure: We were glad they drug us from the presence of the wicked one into the presence of the Righteous One! In His presence we learned that, 'No weapon that is formed against thee shall prosper!'" (See Daniel 3.)

Two are better than one, because they have a good return for their labor: If either of them falls down, one can help the other up. But pity anyone who falls and has no one to help them up (ECCLESIASTES 4:9-10 NIV).

———◦———

What we all need is the unique gift of acceptance. Most of us fear the bitter taste of rejection, but perhaps worse than rejection is the naked pain that attacks an exposed heart when a relationship is challenged by some struggle.

Suppose I share my heart with someone who betrays me, and I am wounded again? The distress of betrayal can become a wall that insulates us, but it also isolates us from those around us. There are good reasons for being protective and careful. Love is always a risk. Yet I still suggest that the risk is worth the reward!

Communication becomes needless between people who need no audible speech. Their speech is the soft pat on a shoulder. Their communication is a concerned glance when all is not well with you. If you have ever sunken down into the rich lather of a real covenant relationship, then you are wealthy.

The Lord said to Moses: "Bring me seventy of Israel's elders who are known to you as leaders and officials among the people. Have them come to the tent of meeting, that they may stand there with you (NUMBERS 11:16 NIV).

---·◦·---

The Body of Christ places a great deal of emphasis on the process of mentoring. The concept of mentoring is scriptural and effective; however, many of us have gone to extremes. Instead of teaching young people to pursue God, they are running amuck looking for someone to to pour into them.

Not everyone is mentored as Joshua was—under the firm hand of a strong leader. Some, like Moses, are prepared by the workings of the manifold wisdom of God. They receive mentoring through circumstances that God ordains to accomplish an end result.

Regardless of which describes your ascent to greatness, it is still God who *"works in you both to will and to do"* (Phil 2:13). When you understand this, you appreciate the people or the methods God used, but ultimately praise the God whose masterful ability to conduct has crescendoed in the finished product of a man or woman of God.

And if anyone thinks that he knows anything, he knows nothing yet as he ought to know. But if anyone loves God, this one is known by Him (I CORINTHIANS 8:2-3).

---·•◦•·---

You need new meditations to dwell in your heart by faith, for your life will ultimately take on the direction of your thinking.

Many weaknesses, such as procrastination and laziness, are just draperies that cover up poor self-esteem and a lack of motivation. They are often symptoms of the subconscious avoiding the risk of failure.

God creates by speaking, but He speaks out of His own thoughts. Since God's Word says *"For out of the abundance of the heart the mouth speaks"* (Matt. 12:34), we go beyond the mouth to bring correction to the words we speak. We have to begin with the thoughts we think.

I pray that somehow the Spirit will reveal where you need Him to heal your thinking so you can possess what God wants you to have. Then you will be able to fully enjoy what He has given you. Many people have the blessing and still don't enjoy it because they conquered every foe except the enemy within!

And let us consider one another to provoke unto love and to good works (HEBREWS 10:24 KJV).

Children understand the rich art of relationship. They are often angry, but their anger quickly dissipates in the glaring sunshine of a fresh opportunity to laugh and jest a day away. The hearts of most adults, however, have been blackened by unforgiveness. They will hold a club of remembered infractions against one another for long periods of time, perhaps for a lifetime. There is a vacancy in the hearts of most people that causes them to be narrow and superficial. This vacancy is the vast gap between casual relationships and intimate attachments. It is the gift of friendship that should fill the gap between these wide designated points of human relationship.

Since there is no blood to form the basis of relativity between friends, the bond must exist through some other mode of reality. A commonality is needed to anchor the relationship of two individuals. However, this bond may exist in an area that outsiders would never understand, but thank God their confusion doesn't dilute the intensity of admiration that exists between true friends. Dare to be a friend!

Him God has exalted to His right hand to be Prince and Savior, to give repentance to Israel and forgiveness of sins (ACTS 5:31).

---◆○◆---

Change is a gift from God. It is given to the person who finds himself too far removed from what he feels destiny has ordained for him. Don't assume that real change occurs without struggle and prayer.

The Bible calls change repentance. Repentance is God's gift to a struggling heart who wants to find himself. Without the Holy Spirit's help you can search and search and still not find repentance. The Lord will show the place of repentance only to those who hunger and thirst after righteousness. The Spirit of God can lead you into a place of renewal that, on your own, you would not find. I believe it was this kind of grace that made John Newton record, "It was grace that taught my heart to fear and grace my fears relieved. How precious did that grace appear the hour I first believed" ("Amazing Grace," early American melody). When God gives you the grace to make changes that you know you couldn't do with your own strength, it becomes precious to you.

And let us consider how we may spur one another on toward love and good deeds (HEBREWS 10:24 NIV).

———•○•———

The extent of damage that mortals can do to the upright is limited by the purposes of God. What a privilege it is to know and understand this in your heart. It destroys the constant paranoia that restricts many of us from exploring possible friendships and covenant relationships. Any time you make an investment, there is the possibility of a loss. But there is a difference between being hurt and being altered or destroyed.

You belong to God, and He watches over you every day. He monitors your affairs, and acts as your protection. Sometimes He opens doors (we always get excited about God opening doors). But the same God who opens doors also closes doors. I am, perhaps, more grateful for the doors He has closed in my life than I am for the ones He has opened. Had I been allowed to enter some of the doors He closed, I would surely have been destroyed! God doesn't intend for every relationship to flourish. There are some human cliques and social groups in which He doesn't want you to be included!

You will show me the path of life; in Your presence is fullness of joy; at Your right hand are pleasures forevermore (PSALM 16:11).

———•◦•———

H ave you begun your search for a closer manifestation of His grace? Your search alone is worship. When you seek Him, it suggests that you value Him and recognize His ability. The staggering, faulty steps of a seeker are far better than the stance of the complacent. He is not far away. He is in the furnace, moving in the ashes. Look closer. He is never far from the seeker who is on a quest to be in His presence.

Job said that God works on the left hand! The right hand in the Bible symbolizes power and authority. That's why Christ is seated on the right side of God (see Mark 16:19). "Right hand" means power. If you were to search for God, you would look on the right hand. Granted, He is on the right hand. He is full of authority, but His strength is made perfect in weakness (see 2 Cor. 12:9). He displays His glory in the ashes of human frailty. He works on the left hand.

And to the angel of the church in Philadelphia write, "These things says He who is holy, He who is true, 'He who has the key of David, He who opens and no one shuts, and shuts and no one opens' (REVELATION 3:7).

The letter to the Philadelphia church, the church of brotherly love, basically ends with the words, "I am the One who closes doors." The art to surviving painful moments is living in the "yes" zone. We need to learn to respond to God with a yes when the doors are open, and a yes when they are closed. Our prayer must be: I trust Your decisions, Lord; and I know that if this relationship is good for me, You will allow it to continue. I know that if the door is closed, it is also for my good. So I say "yes" to You as I go into this relationship. I appreciate brotherly love, and I still say "yes" if You close the door.

This is the epitome of a trust that is seldom achieved, but is to be greatly sought after. In so doing, you will be able to savor companionship without the fear of reprisal!

For you know that afterward, when he wanted to inherit the blessing, he was rejected, for he found no place for repentance, though he sought it diligently with tears (HEBREWS 12:17).

———•○•———

Brother Esau sought for the place of repentance and could not secure it. To be transformed is to be changed. If you are not moving into your divine purpose, you desperately need to repent. If God wants you to change, it is because He wants you to be prepared for what He desires to do next in your life. Get ready; the best is yet to come.

In Romans 12:2 we are instructed not to be conformed to this world. Literally, it says we are not to be conformed to the same *pattern* of this world. We are to avoid using those standards as a pattern for our progress. On a deeper level God is saying, "Do not use the same pattern of the world to measure success or to establish character and values." The term "world" in Greek is *aion* (Strong's #G165), which refers to ages. Do not allow the pattern of the times you are in to become the pattern that shapes your inward person.

The Lord works out everything to its proper end— even the wicked for a day of disaster (PROVERBS 16:4 NIV).

———•○•———

Great growth doesn't come into your life through mountaintop experiences. Great growth comes through the valleys and low places where you feel limited and vulnerable. The time God is really moving in your life may seem to be the lowest moment you have ever experienced. God is working on you, your faith and your character, when the blessing is delayed. The blessing is the reward that comes after you learn obedience through the things you suffered while waiting for it.

The prerequisite of the mountain is the valley. If there is no valley, there is no mountain. After you've been through this process a few times, you begin to realize that the valley is only a sign that with a few more steps, you'll be at the mountain again! So just hold on!

If you've been through a period that didn't seem to have the slightest stirring and God seems to stay still, the answer is no! God hasn't forgotten. Sometimes He moves openly. But sometimes He moves silently, working in the shadows. You can't see Him, but He is working!

And we know that all things work together for good for those who love God, to those who are the called according to His purpose (ROMANS 8:28).

———•○•———

I f no good can come out of a relationship or situation, then God will not allow it. There must be an inner awareness within your heart, a deep knowledge that God is in control and that He is able to reverse the adverse. When we believe in His sovereignty, we can overcome every humanly induced trial because we realize that they are divinely permitted. He orchestrates them in such a way that the things that could have paralyzed us only motivate us.

Even in the most harmonious of relationships there are injuries and adversity. If you live in a cocoon, you will miss all the different levels of love God has for you. God allows different people to come into your life to accomplish His purposes. Your friends are ultimately the ones who will help you become all that God wants you to be in Him. When you consider it in that light, you have many friends—some of them expressed friends, and some implied friends.

To be made new in the attitude of your minds
(EPHESIANS 4:23 NIV).

———————◈◦◈———————

Many individuals in the Body of Christ are persevering without progressing. They wrestle with areas that have been conformed to the world instead of transformed. It is imperative that, while we keep our mode of expression, we understand that transformation doesn't come from inspiration! Transformation takes place in the mind.

The Bible teaches that we are to be renewed by the transforming of our minds (see Rom. 12:2; Eph. 4:23). Only the Holy Spirit knows how to renew the mind. The struggle we have inside us is with our self-perception. Generally our perception of ourselves is affected by those around us. Our early opinion of ourselves is deeply affected by the opinions of the authoritative figures in our formative years. If our parents tend to neglect or ignore us, it tears at our self-worth. Eventually, though, we mature to the degree where we can walk in the light of our own self-image, without it being diluted by the contributions of others.

To appoint unto them that mourn in Zion, to give unto them beauty for ashes, the oil of joy for mourning, the garment of praise for the spirit of heaviness; that they might be called trees of righteousness, the planting of the Lord, that he might be glorified (ISAIAH 61:3 KJV).

———●○●———

The Church is a place where you can come broken and disgusted, and be healed, delivered, and set free in the name of Jesus. Jesus said, *"The Spirit of the Lord is upon Me, because He has anointed Me to preach the gospel to the poor; He has sent Me to heal the broken-hearted, to proclaim liberty to the captives and recovery of sight to the blind, to set at liberty those who are oppressed"* (Luke 4:18).

You may have thought that you would never rejoice again. God declares that you can have freedom in Him—now! The joy that He brings can be restored to your soul. He identifies with your pain and suffering. He knows what it is like to suffer abuse at the hands of others. Yet He proclaims joy and strength. He will give you the garment of praise instead of the spirit of heaviness.

The Lord is with me; I will not be afraid. What can mere mortals do to me? (PSALM 118:6 NIV)

———————◆◦◆———————

God has used certain "friends" and their negativity to accomplish His will for our lives. Now, because our ultimate goal is to please Him, we must widen our definition of friendship to include the betrayer if the betrayal ushered us into the next step of God's plan for our lives.

There are some friends who were actually instrumental in my blessing, although they never really embraced or affirmed me as a person! They played a crucial part in my well-being. These kinds of "friends" are the "Judas sector" that exists in the life of every child of God.

Every child of God not only has, but also desperately needs, a "Judas" to carry out certain aspects of divine providence in his life! Although Peter was certainly more amiable and admirable, Judas was the one God selected to usher in the next step of the process. Sometimes your friends are the ones who can cause you the most pain. They wound you and betray you, but through their betrayal God's will can be executed in your life.

REFLECTIONS

_____
_____
_____
_____
_____
_____
_____
_____
_____
_____
_____
_____
_____
_____
_____
_____
_____
_____
_____
_____
_____
_____